Praise for

⋈ HARVEST ⋈

"In *Harvest*, Max Watman chronicles a year spent trying to eat dishes only made from scratch—proof that,
in cooking as in travel, the journey itself is its own
amazing story."   —*Conde Nast Traveler*

"On the surface, *Harvest* is about food . . . [but a] deeper
examination reveals that, *Harvest* is also about family
and friendship and the role of food in those relationships."
                                   —Shannon Morgan,
                    Washington Independent Review of Books

"Whether it's a ripe camembert, a just-caught striped bass
or a homemade bresaola-of-Bubbles (his steer), Max Watman has the descriptive and narrative power to make the
outer limits of the food world seem both magnificently
rare and dangerously explorable and appealing."
                        —Matt Lee and Ted Lee, authors of
                        The Lee Bros. Southern Cookbook

Also by Max Watman

Chasing the White Dog:
An Amateur Outlaw's Adventures in Moonshine

Race Day:
A Spot on the Rail with Max Watman

HARVEST

Field Notes from a Far-Flung Pursuit of Real Food

MAX WATMAN

W. W. Norton & Company

New York • London

For information about permission to reproduce selections
from this book, write to Permissions, W. W. Norton & Company, Inc.,
500 Fifth Avenue, New York, NY 10110

Beef-cut chart © 2013 by Katherine Eastland Messenger.
E-mails from John Whiteside reprinted with permission.

For information about special discounts for
bulk purchases, please contact W. W. Norton Special Sales
at specialsales@wwnorton.com or 800-233-4830

Manufacturing by Courier Westford
Book design by Charlotte Staub
Production manager: Louise Mattarelliano

Library of Congress Cataloging-in-Publication Data
Watman, Max.
Harvest : field notes from a far-flung pursuit of real food / Max Watman. —
First edition.
pages cm
Includes bibliographical references.
ISBN 978-0-393-06302-8 (hardcover)
1. Natural foods. 2. Self-reliant living. 3. Family farms—Hudson River Valley
Region (N.Y. and N.J.) 4. Watman, Max—Homes and haunts. I. Title.
TX369.W38 2014
641.3'02—dc23 2013036810

ISBN 978-0-393-35083-8 pbk.

W. W. Norton & Company, Inc.
500 Fifth Avenue, New York, N.Y. 10110
www.wwnorton.com

W. W. Norton & Company Ltd.
Castle House, 75/76 Wells Street, London W1T 3QT

1 2 3 4 5 6 7 8 9 0

For Rachael
—with love and oysters

CONTENTS

⚒ HARVEST ⚒

CHAPTER ONE

Yellow Tag 879

I CALLED MY STEER BUBBLES. He was bred at Wolf Creek Farm in Wolftown, Virginia, in Madison County. As befits a resident of those rolling hills, he was the product of careful breeding—a mix of Black Angus, Red Angus, and Polled Hereford. I bought him when he was a year old. In his ear was a yellow tag with the number 879. He weighed in at 675 pounds.

My plan: buy a steer. I'd start with an animal, he would graze for about a year, and then he'd be food. It turns out that this, the simplest plan ever concocted, just one short step beyond hunting and gathering, a series of events that mirror what people have been doing since cattle were domesticated, was not at all straightforward.

First of all, I had to figure out where to put a steer once I bought him.

Although my yard doesn't seem big enough for cattle, it is. My plot is about 0.11 of an acre, a total of 4,791 square feet. I'd say about half of that is built on, leaving 2,395 square feet of potential grazing land. Admittedly, I call some of that square footage "flower beds," and there are a fair number of chairs and tables, and I'd like to leave room for the pizza oven I'm going to build. Cattle on a concentrated animal feeding operation (a CAFO, commonly called a feedlot)—where the beef that is for sale in the supermarket comes from—is "finished" (i.e., raised through the last months of its life like a duck on a foie gras farm,* fed on corn until it jiggles and wiggles with the unctuous fat that we've come to expect) on about 30 square feet per animal. My yard is big enough to carry seventy-nine beeves. I'm not saying it's big enough to run a cattle operation. I don't think I have enough space for calving, or heifers, but with some modifications—a pit that I could fill up with shit and a hopper I could fill up with grain—I could keep one steer and fatten him up according to the standards that are in practice for the majority of farmed cattle. I'd even have room left for the pizza oven.

For any number of reasons—marital stability, resale value, and local laws being at the top of the list—it's a bad idea, and I didn't entertain it for long. I probably spent only a day musing on what the bellowing of a steer in a small pen in the middle of a village might do for the local ambience. I spent, all told, only an hour and a half calculating the viability of a sideline petting zoo and cattle-riding center for the local children.

After I dismissed the idea of the yard cow, I asked myself what I wanted to achieve. Pacing off my yard and imagining seventy-nine head of cattle arrayed therein is enough in itself to put one off of supermarket beef. A fully grown animal commands about twenty-one square feet. It doesn't take Temple Grandin to tell me that a steer might be healthier and happier with a little more room to roam

---

*It's worth noting that ducks and geese are, at least, natural eaters of grain. Cattle are not.

than a third of its own mass. That'd be, basically, as if I had to live for three months in a crowded rush-hour subway car, during which time all of the passengers crapped on the floor and were fed nothing but huge ice cream sundaes laced with antibiotics. Betty Fussell wrote a book called *Raising Steaks* about the cattle business. (It's not all bad news in those pages—she likes beef, and she isn't arguing for the end of meat eating or the dissolution of the industry.) It becomes clear, however, that the segmentation of the supply chain—the division of labor that is so much a part of what the late stages of our Industrial Revolution have wrought—doesn't do us any favors. As Fussell writes, "The traditional industrial beef chain moves in sequence: The cow-calf person sells to a backgrounder (or yearling operator) who sells to a feedlot who sells to a packer who sells to a wholesaler who sells to a retailer." When each segment of that chain is a separate entity, it maximizes profits in ways that do not necessarily benefit the other segments of the chain. What's more, although this cannot be said of individual cattlemen—despite sensational news stories to the contrary, no one cares more about cattle than those who raise, herd, and mind them—the system itself is not concerned with the health or wellbeing of the animal. The business of the system is moving the cows through it, and each segment's priority is getting the animal to the next stage.

It should be taken for granted that only at the retail segment, the last stop, are the consumers taken into consideration at all.

Imagine if the truth were immediately evident: imagine if that on one's way to the supermarket, one first drove a causeway across a lagoon of liquified manure, and then took a twisting road through a feedlot, past the conveyor belt of cattle being killed, and then, perhaps, through a sort of car-wash tunnel where the rapidly separated carcasses were being sawn and ground up—how many boxes of hamburger would be sold by the time the customer reached the store?

I wanted a freezer full of beef because I love it, and I don't want it to come from a system that doesn't care about me or the animal that is going to feed me. Since I've nixed the yard cow—*note to wife: I've really nixed it, Rachael; you can relax*—the next obvious answer would be that I simply buy my beef from a better source, such as the farmers' market or a boutique butcher shop. Two problems present themselves with this solution. The first is that I can't afford it. Despite the well-advertised and rightly argued truth that the cheap meat arrayed in the supermarket is a false economy, the fact remains that within my own household this false economy is the actual one. I understand that millions upon millions of dollars are spent and shuffled to allow corporate beef pricing to remain rock-bottom,* but that doesn't change

---

*I cannot calculate the real cost of corporate farming, and I haven't been able to find anyone who has done it. It looms as one of the real issues we'll need to figure out as a society. It starts with farm subsidies that keep the cost of large-scale corn production in check, and it tentacles out in many ways. The environmental costs are staggering, and they are all externalized. Big Ag is not responsible for costs incurred by algae blooms in water, or by fish kills, or by the hypoxic dead zone in the Gulf of Mexico (to which the largest contributor is agricultural runoff). Nor are corporate farms responsible for the infections and deaths caused by antibiotic-resistant bacteria, despite the fact that 80 percent of the antibiotics that are dispensed in America are given to livestock, usually at a trickle, which seems designed to strengthen bacteria. The costs of hospitalizations, doctor visits, and drug research all add up. According to a CDC report, "S. Aureus and MRSA Surveillance Summary: MRSA Infections," there were an estimated 278,000 hospitalizations in the United States to treat drug-resistant MRSA infections in 2005. We haven't even

the fact that I have to walk into a store and take money out of my pocket to buy the beef, and there's a big differential between three-dollar-a-pound supermarket brisket and thirteen-dollar-a-pound brisket at the farmers' market. Just because you opt out of the system doesn't mean that the hidden costs are returned to you. (It's a bit like school taxes in this sense: you're paying the public school tax whether or not you decide to send your kid to private school.) So if I've decided that I can no longer participate in a sprawling, unjust system of factory farming that despoils the land, tortures the animals, and breeds superbugs, then I must find a solution* that doesn't involve a double-digit-per-pound premium.

The second problem is more subtle. I want to get my hands dirty. If I were to work toward making enough money to buy whatever beef I wanted, I might succeed at it. I trust the farmers at the market and the butchers at the little shops; I appreciate what they are doing, but I'd still be buying food that I didn't have anything to do with.

When I was nine years old, or just on the cusp, I got

---

gotten into the production of greenhouse gases, or the simple through costs of maintaining highways—with taxpayer money—so that Big Ag can drive trucks full of products around the country. When you start folding all these costs into the price of a steak, it seems that it really costs $900 a pound. When you think about cost in terms of damage, in terms of what it might really cost us to continue this way, it starts to look as if it might simply cost us everything.

*Many readers will, at this moment, wonder why I don't stop eating meat. There are some compelling arguments for vegetarianism, but none of them quite make it for me. I believe that the world is divided into prey animals and predators, and that I am a predator. I know that cattle convert marginal land—that is, land that can't be farmed for vegetables— into usable calories and that they do this with remarkable efficiency. I also like cows and know that were we to remove the value from the cow by not eating them, they would soon disappear.

very picky about food (about everything, really; my mom reminds me that I wore the same khaki-colored corduroy suit to school every day). I insisted on packing a peanut-butter-and-jelly sandwich for lunch, and I decided I wouldn't eat chicken. It must have driven my folks crazy. In the spring of 1980, my parents and I were in a car accident. We were driving in our big Econoline van out to the Eastern Shore of Maryland when a drunk jumped his Mercedes over the median strip of the highway and slammed into us. One does not forget car accidents: my mom and I were in the back of the van, lounging on the bed we'd built there, and my dad said, "Hold on!" He slowed down, but the impact shot me forward to the back of his seat. The force was so great that I remember thinking, *Why can't I stop myself?* It was as if I kept being shoved forward. Then we were lying on a grassy hill, everyone bleeding. The vehicles were obscured by steam and smoke; the air was filled with the horrible smell of fuel, scorched metal, and ferric blood. I came out okay—a Mepps lure stuck in my head, and the tip of my tongue bit off. My parents, though, were pretty beat up. They both had fractured ribs and perforated lungs. My mom had a laceration on her scalp. They recovered but needed a long convalescence. I remember them in bed together, reading and blowing into a device that looked like a snorkel to see how high in the device's tube they could float a ball.

I helped out around the house while my parents healed. A family friend mailed me a care package of cleaning supplies, including a scrubber with a handle you could fill up with soap and water, and some gloves with scrubby sponges on the fronts. I was thrilled with my role as caretaker and suggested that with a little instruction, I could make dinner. Through a haze of Percocet, they gave me orders: Preheat the oven, unwrap a chicken, remove the giblets, rinse the bird, and pat it dry. Rub it inside and out with salt and pepper, put it on a rack, slide it into the hot oven, and set the timer. Don't trust the timer, and by all means don't rely upon the stupid little plastic dart that is supposed to pop up when the bird is done. (I'm sure that my father rose through the murky opioid depths to insist that by the time the button had popped up, the chicken would be irrevocably overcooked.) I was to baste, but only occasionally. I should jiggle the leg and feel how it first grabbed tight and then began to give. When I thought it might be done, I should pierce the thigh with a skewer—if the juices ran clear, the bird was cooked. Our stove was electric and that deep mustard yellow color that was popular at the time—also popular, ironically, as a color for Mercedes.

Although my family was at the nascence of our true journey into the depths of food obsession, food was already important. My folks had already run a catering business. We hadn't fallen off the deep end yet, but dinner was not a thing that was taken lightly in the Watman house. And now it was mine to make.

It was a gas. I loved the bulb baster and the way the heady aromas filled the air. I loved the blast of heat on my face when I opened the oven door. For all our cultural, mythopoetical baggage about the warmth of the hearth, the truth is that the hearth isn't warm—it's hot. It's warm later, when all the bellies are full and everyone is satiated. While you are cooking, the hearth is still torrid and the oven is hot. As a cook, you confront a radiant warning that you will be burned if you proceed, and you disregard it. And, of course, you do get burned. Right now, as I type, I can look down at my hands and see a raw arc of flesh across the top of my wrist where I brushed up against the mouth of my oven while reaching into it.* It's a primal poetry as real as any: I saw the fire, felt its heat, and reached inside.

The timer was whirring along, and I was jabbing a skewer into the thigh, probably every forty-five seconds or so. By the time the crisped skin snapped in just the right way and the luscious fat spurted clear from the thigh, I was forever changed. I had turned a corner. I was proud as hell. My folks loved the meal, and so did I.

I'd learned something, and I'd made something. I had been, just the day before, a choosy consumer, a passive participant. Now I was a producer. I felt it. It was as if I'd gone off into the woods to find my spirit animal and returned to the tribe a man.

Doing things counts. Getting your hands dirty is real.

We have invested a lot, culturally, in smarter shopping. The comedian David Cross has a joke in which he goes to Whole Foods where he is buying some plastic wrap. Next to the house brand of plastic wrap there is another brand: If You Care. "Oh, come *on!*" he cries. "I *care*. I'm already in Whole Foods! Leave me alone!" But what has he done?

Let's use, as an example, the closing symbol of *Casablanca*. After Ingrid Bergman flies away and the cops haul off the murdered Nazi with the instructions to round

---

*When I started cooking professionally, I cut and burned myself a lot. Gradually, I came to understand that if you were focused and careful, it didn't happen. But then, of course, you are not always paying attention. As a home cook, I've found that I don't get hurt in the kitchen very much. Every once in a while, because I'm trying to have a conversation while I'm chopping broccolini, I cut through the nail of my finger and whack off a good eighth of an inch. Or my wrist brushes the hot rim of the oven because I was trying to drink a glass of Crémant while I was pulling out a roast.

up the usual suspects, Claude Rains, playing the chief of police, throws away a bottle of Vichy water in a symbolic rejection of the occupying forces. Pretend, for a moment, that Vichy water was more than a symbol—that the purchasing of Vichy water actually funded the occupation. Let us also pretend, perhaps, that there was another competing bottle of mineral water and that this second brand siphoned money into the coffers of the resistance. Certainly one's refusal to buy Vichy water is a step in the right direction. It is still, however, a negative value.* It is value gained by *not* doing something. More value would be gained by purchasing the competing resistance water. By eschewing one and embracing the other, one would have taken a pretty big step in support of the resistance. None of it, however, gets anywhere near the value of *actually fighting in the resistance.* No amount of shopping can substitute for the grind of the dirt under the soles of your boots.

But of course, I can't put a cow in my yard.

So I called my friend Nathan Carter. His yard is a farm. Could I put a cow in *his* yard? I worry, sometimes, that my friends are all sitting around grinning knowingly, sending text messages to one another: "Max thinks we should all

* "Negative value" doesn't mean that you subtract. It is used, mostly by ethics philosophers, to indicate a value that is gained by not doing something. In the consideration of individual rights, for example, the freedom of speech is a "negative" right because one's duty lies only in *not* impeding another's exercising of that right. It is also important in household economics. By working at home, I am available to pick up our son West after school, which means that we don't have to pay someone else to do it. These values should not be underestimated. When West was very young, I was offered a job in New York. I figured out that between the child care, commuting, and sundry other costs, we would hit a positive cash flow at $79,000. The first $79,000, in other words, would move right through me to someone else.

buy a boat." (Didn't do it.) "Max wants me to come help cut down a vine he found out in the woods and put it in the truck so he can make an archway out of it." (It was beautiful until a particularly strong gust of wind snapped the weakening bough, and the arch flopped over in the grass.) "Max just fed us a bunch of meat he cured himself; waiting to see how sick we'll get." (They didn't get sick.)

Nathan seemed singularly prepared for the project at the time. He is the farm manager for Graves Mill Farm—664 acres of hilly, rolling country, the best Virginia has to offer. He didn't even flinch.

On the face of it, Nathan Carter would fall into the much-reported-on category of the "hipster farmer." This coterie has been presented as new, but it is not. An early urban farmer, Bolton Hall was cultivating city plots and inspiring people to go back to the land in the first decade of the twentieth century. It was 1972 when memoirist Joyce Maynard, then an eighteen-year-old freshman at Yale, wrote an article for the *New York Times Magazine* about the boys she'd known at Exeter who had begun wearing overalls and listening to country music and telling the college placement counselors that they were "going to study weaving in Norway, to be shepherds in the Alps, deckhands on a fishing boat or—most often—farmers." People have been "returning" to farming for ages—ever since there was anything else to do, ever since the first kid walked off the farm. It's in the New Testament, after all, for what is the prodigal son but a hipster kid who fled the farm to hit the big city and dance in the bright lights only to return? He's the original gangster.

The popularity of farming, at least among those not born to it, seems to be cyclical. Nathan was an early adopter on this latest wave. It caught us all by surprise, but the surprise didn't last. It was one of those pronouncements like when a friend comes out of the closet or a writer turns out one of those lovely passages where by the end of the arc you feel you've known his conclusion forever.

That doesn't mean that when Nathan called to tell me the news I wasn't surprised. I was standing in the kitchen (where the telephone was), looking out my window over the leaves of the top edge of Riverside Park, just north of Grant's Tomb. He was calling from Brooklyn. He was moving upstate, he announced, to work on a dairy farm. I (predictably) suggested a party. He said there was no time. He was going tomorrow.

When I met Nathan, we were maybe twenty-two years old, and Rachael and I lived in Richmond. Nathan was there when I cooked my first bouillabaisse at what counts as the first dinner party I ever threw. Obviously, we'd eaten with friends—stir-fries and big pots of spaghetti—but there is a sea change when you say to yourself that you are going to throw a party, and you work hard on it. We hosted a dozen people in our little one-bedroom apartment. It was a crumbling thing, plaster falling out of the ceiling and a back porch we called California because it was only a matter of time until it fell off. Rachael and I ate at a rickety little porcelain enamel table in the kitchen. We set up the tables in our middle room and covered them with cloth. It's hard to imagine how poor we were at the time and how reckless we were with our money for that party. We were young and making nothing. We spent $400 on a dinner party. We needed it. We wanted candles but had nothing to set them in. So we bought little candle bases of colored glass. I hit up the fish dealer that delivered to the restaurant where I worked at the time and got some fish frames to make the base of the stock from which we'd make the bouilla-baisse. We bought a dozen loaves of excellent bread and put out a couple of infused oils, a salmon pâté, a scallop mousse, and a tapenade—things we could all just smear on bread and eat. We bought magnums of Montepulciano d'Abruzzo.

None of us had had a dinner party like this before. None of us had been at one of our homes eating fine, orches-trated food. We were mesmerized.

"I had never eaten like that at all," Nathan told me recently when I asked him if he remembered it. "Nobody I'd ever known had cooked like that. I grew up eating burgers at my aunt's house. I'd never eaten in restaurants. Pâté? What's that? Food was sustenance, and it became something pleasurable. That party laid the groundwork for me to understand what food is."

The bouillabaisse. When the intoxicating hit of saffron and rouille came around, everyone was already rolling on crazy flavors and the best wine—or at least the best wine we could buy. It was one of those dinner parties that takes off, like a good rock-and-roll show or good drugs when everyone loses sight of their anxiety and everyone is laughing and totally together. Sometimes I think of dinner parties as that plane that NASA uses to practice weight-lessness. There's the ascent, which can be a struggle, engines whining and screaming, people tense and unsure of what is going to come next, and if the engines don't stall and the weather plays along, you reach the apex, you tip the plane, and everyone rises out of their seat and floats. We'd started something.

Our big group ate together religiously, at least once a week, with a rotating cast of extras. There would be whole fish, crab cakes, handmade tortillas. We would play croquet in Chimborazo Park and drink beer, and then retire to someone's house to eat orecchiette with Gorgonzola and peas, or huge piles of steamed mussels.

We got very lucky, because when it came time to move away, we managed to continue the party. Our friend David Clark had been accepted at Pratt, I was going to Columbia University, and Nathan was talking about film school and had been accepted at the New School for Social Research. Our lazy, hot afternoons of croquet were replaced with long subway rides and gritty East Village dive bars, but we kept on eating together.

Nathan had his hipster cred squared away, but of course there was misery that came along with it. While attending classes, he worked in the kitchen of a bar in Williamsburg where the bathrooms regularly smelled of crack smoke due to the proclivities of the dishwashers, and where the owner had whipped him through a death march in search of the perfect brownie. He'd cooked dozens of different brownie recipes, scouring cookbooks and working from scratch, only to have them dismissed. Finally, disgusted, he bought a box of brownie mix; the owner declared it perfect.

He stole a weekend away with his girlfriend, Shannon, who would become his wife, and while they were upstate, they saw a bucolic dairy farm in a hollow in the Catskills. I've been there, and the morning sun slanting into that little valley and burning off the mist to reveal a grazing herd of Holsteins is among the most beautiful things I've ever seen. It's bewitching, even if you haven't been mixing brownies from a box and working with crackheads. If you had, it would sing like a chorus of choir boys, beckoning you to greater beauty.

They put the farm in the rearview mirror and drove the

narrow mountain roads to Windham, where they settled into their rented cottage. Nathan bought a local paper and looked through the want ads without purpose, curious about what people in the Catskills did. One listing read "Dairy Farm, Labor" and gave a phone number.

He showed the ad to Shannon, and they joked about how funny it would be if it were the very farm they'd just looked at. I can see the scene: coffee and fried eggs and good country light and the two of them smiling and glowing. She said to call and see—maybe it was. When he did, a man with a thick Dutch accent ("Which I'd never heard before in my life," Nathan said) told him to come around at seven in the morning to talk.

Nathan's farming experience was slight. He'd spent a chunk of his Texas childhood living in one of the old houses on a beef farm. His father worked in Austin during the week, and on the weekends, he'd earn the rent by taking care of the farm—the typical routine of mending fences and mowing grass. At harvest time, he'd drive a combine.

Nathan's grandfather owned a hundred acres outside of Rockdale, Texas, and kept a small beef operation going there. "We used to go out there and hang out on that farm and play and look at the cattle."

Still larking, Nathan went to meet the dairy farmer. "I showed up at 6:45, of course, and he said, 'I like you already. I've never had anyone be on time—for anything.' We walked through the dairy, where they were milking. We went and saw the heifer calves. He drove me up to the tenant house."

They were leaning on the sides of the pickup truck bed—the best country moments happen leaning against trucks—and the farmer asked Nathan what he thought. Nathan wasn't exactly happy working and going to school in the city, but he did like the music scene and had lots of friends. He certainly hadn't planned on leaving.

"I think it's great!" he said.

"Well, what do you think about three hundred bucks a week, and this house?" asked the farmer.

"I think it sounds great."

"When can you start?"

"I'll drive to Brooklyn right now and get my stuff; I'll start tomorrow."

"Oh no you're not. You have a job in the city, right? You give those people some notice."

And so Nathan became a farmer. Of course it was the same farm they'd seen. This is one of those stories, after all, where fate seems like a line of dominoes waiting to be tipped. He was up there at the dairy for two and a half years.

He and Shannon got married, migrated south to Virginia, and had three kids. He held a couple of jobs at bigger industrial farms, where he gradually grew interested in moving away from the standard grain-fed process. He steered a cattle operation into farming more responsibly, not because he'd brought idealism into the scenario but because it made sense. Nathan came to see it as a choice: care for pastures and infrastructure, or shovel corn and care for sick animals. He went on to manage the feed program at a large dairy, which won Virginia Dairy of the Year in 2007 because of his efforts.

I asked if as he had grown into that sort of farming he'd come to relate to the wave of socially/enviro-conscious young people that are taking up farming.

"Not really," he said, laughing. "They're trying to save the world. . . . They're very involved in making the world a better place, and I'm not into that. I just want to be fair to the customers and to the chefs and to the animals. I just want to enjoy myself."

Nathan finally found a spot in which he could do just that when he hired on at Graves Mill and started raising lambs. Richmond—a mere ninety miles away and largely untouched from a marketing standpoint—seemed like the perfect place to peddle the meat. He met with some success and with some friction. He was surprised to learn how dearly chefs there clung to the bottom line, telling him that they could get lamb from Sysco for a buck or two cheaper than his.

"They didn't seem to get it a lot of the time. They didn't understand that they could just pass that cost right along to the customer and the customer might be happy to hear that they had this lamb that was walking around on a pasture a couple of days ago, ninety miles away." He'd hear, "This just isn't that kind of place; our customers don't care."

"Maybe that's true," he said. "Maybe customers don't know what that big silver Sysco truck means. You and I do, because we worked in restaurants, but do people get it? Do people understand that the lamb was sitting, frozen, in a container on a ship all the way from New Zealand?"

He was laughing and shaking his head, but it had been a real hurdle for him. He sold his lamb at the farmers' market in Madison, where he had stalwart customers, and worked to educate Richmond's chefs. He sold little pieces at deep discounts to demonstrate how much better lamb could be. He had some success. His old boss at Mamma Zu, a raucously fun Italian restaurant in the Oregon Hill neighborhood of Richmond, would joyfully buy whole animals, ranting about how all the lamb off of the Sysco truck tasted like cardboard.

Nathan had eighteen good months before the whole thing went to pot. The owners of Graves Mill decided they wanted to move back out West. They put the farm up for sale and halted the business.

Nathan sold most of the stock into auction and got good money for it: "Fifteen cents above the going rate, per pound. People knew I had good stuff, that I'd raised those sheep right."

He was given a handful of sheep as a Christmas bonus. The staff was let go. With no herd to run, he was operationally demoted to caretaker.

Graves Mill leased some pasture to Wolf Creek Farm for grazing, so buying a Wolf Creek steer felt natural, especially since Nathan thought it'd be fun to raise one up to finishing weight.

I drove to Virginia and met John Whiteside, the owner of Wolf Creek Farm. We rode out into the fields in his old Ford. He gave me a good tour, showed me a steer I could have—"I'll weigh him, and I'll mail you an invoice"— and we shook on it.

Back at home, when I told folks that I'd bought a steer, most of them were amused. The question that came up over and over, to my surprise, was whether or not I'd named him. For a while, I explained that naming livestock was a horrible idea. You don't name dinner.

This answer didn't get many laughs.

I was surprised at my cohorts. I'd thought that surely

all these grass-fed-beef-eating farmers' market friends of mine understood the way of the farm. This is the Hudson Valley, right? This is farm-to-table land. But over and over I got, "Did you name him?"

So I said I had. I said I called my steer Bubbles.

⚞ CHAPTER TWO ⚟

Living with Girls

WE NAMED OUR CHICKENS Goldie, Pepper, Karen, and Penguin. Goldie was a Buff Orpington hen, the biggest of the girls and the leader—the top of the pecking order. She was a very good-looking bird, with soft feathers the color of straw—so good looking, in fact, that when I lent her to a neighbor girl who entered her in a country fair, she won a blue ribbon as a perfect example of her breed. I liked to pretend that she lorded this victory over her coop mates. Goldie had been out there in the world. She'd seen things, and she'd taken her prize. She was the most cosmopolitan of the chickens.

Pepper and Penguin were Blue (a color more like slate, really) Ameraucanas, with little pea combs and muffs around their faces; the eggs they laid had pale blue-green shells. Penguin was not much by way of personality, but Pepper was the smartest and most daring of the chickens. She was the one who would hop up onto people's shoulders and was always out of the coop first when I opened the gate to let them run around in the yard. Karen was a Golden Laced Wyandotte. She was lovely to look at but slightly dumber than the rest: she was easily confused by obstacles—she would stand in front of a twig, unable to go around or over it, or she would doubt her ability to squeeze through a door that wasn't open all the way. She liked cozy spaces and seemed to find comfort in a slot between a dense bush and the fence. She was very easy to catch. One got the feeling that Karen was a sweetheart.

Penguin died early, before she was two years old, of what I termed sudden chicken death syndrome—she simply dropped. I walked out to the coop and she was lying in a heap by the watering fount. It was a sad, mysterious moment but very much the sort of thing to which one must be inured. To care for chickens is to carry their corpses. They are vulnerable birds. Insects can beat a chicken in a fair fight if they get themselves organized. The birds are susceptible to all sorts of maladies and mishaps. Most of all, everything likes to eat chickens.

Learning about death is one of the lessons that is said to be delivered early to children who live in agricultural settings, along with a familiarity with where babies come from, and it was a pretty well-timed lesson for my son West, who was four at the time and in the midst of a morbid phase, always asking us to drive around in graveyards and wondering whether people were buried under statues. He took the news of Penguin's demise solemnly and was sad while he digested the information over the course of an hour or so, after which he owned it.

"We used to have four chickens," he told his little friends. His eyebrows would flare, and he'd deliver the closer with appropriate, shivering excitement, playing the part of a lilliputian emcee of the Grand Guignol: "Now we have three because Penguin *died*."

I wanted chickens because I'd had them when I was a kid and because I wanted the eggs. As more people put more chickens in their backyards, some studies have been done on the eggs, and apparently they are not measurably different from grocery store eggs. I can't really bring myself to believe it. They *seem* to taste better. They certainly look better in the pan. The yolks have a vivid color and seem to stand up straight. They act better when being whipped into mayonnaise. But even if our senses are fooling us about the organoleptic qualities of the yard egg and the product of our flocks turns out to be indistiguishable from the flat, pale, runny things at the grocery store, there's still something to crow about. If you take care of the chickens and the space where they live and handle the eggs properly, you have a food that is a marked improvement on the mass-produced egg. It hasn't rolled through filth, and the chicken that laid it isn't ravaged by disease and flush full of chemicals to fight those diseases.

You will also have removed yourself from a system that can only be classified as cruel. The egg battery—the gruesome system of farming that provides most of our eggs—rewards even the slightest investigation with a disturbing vision of a deeply callous system in which the animals are unable to act out their most basic instincts such as roosting or nesting. Battery hens try very hard to find a private space in which to lay eggs, but since their cage is about the size of a piece of paper, they do not succeed.

There's no need for karmic or hygienic squeamishness over a yard egg. A yard egg is a small moral victory.

I built a funky two-level coop. The bottom—the so-called run—gave them dirt and dust to flap around in, and the top gave them space to nest and roost. They had way more space than four chickens need, according to everything I'd read. I built it mostly out of scrap lumber, and I like to joke that the plans were printed on the side of a can of beer, because when I couldn't figure out what I was doing while I was building it—it was 50 percent planned, 50 percent improvised—I would take a step back and stare at my beer until a solution came to me. Rachael painted it red with a white stripe across the door, on which she stenciled a rooster silhouette. I used a roll of copper flashing that was sitting in my basement for no apparent reason to flash the walls. On the whole, it looked spontaneous, but it had a special luster—think Haiti goes Ivy League.

The chickens in my yard seemed happy. They ran around, chased each other, ate bugs. They got carrot trimmings and leaves of cabbage out of the kitchen. This might be a bit of country wisdom I picked up in my youth rather than an actual chicken-raising fact, but care should be taken not to feed them meat, because they will look around and will see that their coop mates are *also* made of meat, and they will eat one another. As I've said, everything likes to eat chickens—even chickens. I've always thought it was like the hungry cartoon character in the old Warner Bros. cartoons who sees another character on a tray, with those little paper tufts on his legs and an apple in his mouth.

The Girls, as the chickens came to be known,* also lent a wonderful vibe to the yard. Big-table backyard dinner parties were enhanced by the chickens clucking around. They made my yard a landscape. They were beautiful to look at and fun to watch. Kids loved them. People would

---

*Calling the chickens "the Girls" led to a small comedy of errors at an annual checkup with West. There's a questionnaire the doctors run through every year, a sort of prescreening for Child Protective Services about guns and lifestyle choices and sudden changes. The doctor asked, "Who lives at your house with you?" to which West answered, "There's my mom, and me, and Dad, and the Girls."

stop at my fence to check them out and ask questions. One little neighborhood girl began referring to our place as "the farm," which was incredibly satisfying. This wasn't just another little house in a quaint town in the Hudson Valley. This was a farm.

I am a writer, which means that my professional activities—at least when I'm at home—involve staring at walls, going to libraries, typing, and rationalizing ever earlier cocktail hours. These are very nonagricultural activities. Having chickens is a bit of an antidote to that. I found that I liked the routine of feeding, cleaning, and filling water founts. I liked the galvanized buckets and scoops. I liked the necessity of the care. It doesn't matter if it's cold, or raining, or you're tired: livestock demands attention. You can't just blow it off. Having things that must be done, no matter what, can be a great boon to those who sit at home and stare at walls and type.

We'd had them for over three years when things went wrong.

I found Goldie dead in the dirt with a broken neck. Something had dug a small hole under the wall of the coop and squeezed in. As the top hen, Goldie had no doubt come down from the roost to do the rooster's job of defending the flock. (I once watched the Girls attack a squirrel that found its way into the coop while the door was open. They dive-bombed him, one after the other, while he ran around in panicked circles.) I assumed the invader this time was a possum, since it hadn't eaten Goldie.

Naming livestock really is a mistake—a morning spent picking up flecks of gore proves it—but I can't pretend the Girls weren't pets. It was a mistake I enjoyed making. Even if they hadn't been elevated above their proper station, to care for a creature is to enter into a contract. I had agreed to shepherd these birds, and now they were being preyed upon. It was my job to defend them. I worked to secure the coop, picking up bricks and flagstones from around the yard to skirt the run and make digging under the walls more difficult. I reinforced the wire.

It wasn't enough. The next invasion came within a month.

Rachael shook me awake before seven on a Friday morning in late October 2010. We would have been up soon anyway, getting West ready for school, rushing around, fixing breakfast for my sister-in-law and her two kids, who had come into town for a long weekend to celebrate Rachael's birthday. It was the sort of break in a daily rhythm—like the telephone ringing at two in the morning—that signifies something amiss. A neighbor, the mother of the little girl who called our place "the farm," had knocked on our door and announced that there was a very good-looking chicken scratching around in a driveway a few houses down, and she was pretty sure it was ours.

I stepped into the chilly dawn, transformed. Looking for livestock in the early morning is something that farmers do. Even though I was on edge—chickens don't like to wander; something had happened—it felt good to be up in the morning with a purpose, seeing my breath in the autumn air, a man with a flock to gather.

I found Karen exactly where my neighbor had said she'd be, in a driveway down the street, and she was weirdly skittish. She didn't usually run from me. To her, I was the rooster and the bringer of treats. She often followed me around, and while she might duck away if I moved up on her too fast, usually she'd simply squat and let me pick her up. Now she was darting about, clucking, nervous. I got Rachael—*I can't catch her; I need help!*—and we cornered her. Rachael scooped her up. Her clucks got louder and louder as we approached the coop. Some beast had dug a hole under the corner big enough for a Scottish terrier to wiggle through, and one side of the coop was completely blown out, all the wire separated from the frame. I put Karen in the bottom and opened the top, looking for Pepper.

It took me a second to realize I'd found her. There wasn't much left. Pepper, or what had been Pepper, was on her back, eviscerated. Her breasts were eaten clean. There was an empty cavity of breastbone, devoid of organ or meat, and her slate blue wings were outstretched against the golden straw on the floor, as if she were making a snow angel. There was a globule of blood. A bit of her head was still attached.

I let Karen out into the yard to walk around—no wonder she didn't want to be in there—and cleaned the mess. By the time I'd replaced the straw bedding in the second level, I was seething, a backyard Achilles: "We will let all this be a thing of the past, and for all our sorrow beat down by force the anger deeply within us. Now I shall go, to overtake that killer of a dear life." Something was going to die for this. I would take revenge. I would keep poor Karen safe, and I would kill whatever was responsible.

I drove to Walmart and bought an air rifle that advertised itself as strong enough to shoot small game. As always, I ran into a couple of neighbors while I was there, and I got a few raised eyebrows for pushing my cart around with a rifle in it. My little Hudson Valley town is split rather clearly between the old Italian and Irish blue-collar families who don't relate to New York City and don't flinch at the sight of a rifle, and the new crop of urban refugees, absurdly well-educated young families, mostly, who write letters to the editor and harbor an aversion to firearms (or in this case, things that resemble firearms).

I have always bridged these two worlds. My day-to-day life is inarguably micropolitan. I find my rabbits in the grocery store, not the hedgerow, and I'm more likely to be seen buying a tiny button of goat's cheese than ammunition. But I was raised in the country, and I have a strong streak of redneck in me.

I spent the rest of the morning taking some target practice up in the woods at my friend C. Russell Muth's house. Russell is a television producer who, when not on location with his small, rowdy, run-and-gun crew, flits back and forth between New York and Los Angeles, as he has for the last fifteen years. But he is, forever in his heart, a child of the Chesapeake, a Marylander, an Old Bay–seasoned good old boy who likes shotguns, dogs, and baseball caps. He lives in a little cottage on a dirt road with his wife, Candace, and his daughter, Jacqueline. In a matter of moments, he and I were back to our roots, twelve-year-old kids looking for things to shoot and laughing in the brisk morning. I had a Styrofoam target brick, and the *thwap* of a hollow-point pellet slapping into it punctuated our talk.

Tell me about the duck, I said. *Thwap*: off bull's-eye, two inches down and an inch and a half to the right. All my shots were grouping there. I was trying to dial in the sight. Sighting in a gun is a slow process. My new air rifle had a scope (which made me feel very cool), and basically, if you put the crosshairs of a scope on a bull's-eye, you should hit it. If you're off, you need to adjust the scope. In this scenario, there's no such thing as being a good or bad shot; it's just math. It's not particularly entertaining stuff, and Russell had taken his bird dog, a Brittany bitch named Hazel, down to Palatine Lake in New Jersey just a few days before for the opening of duck season. They hunted pheasant regularly, but it had been her first duck hunt. I wanted the story to pass the time.

They spent most of the day without ducks.

Thwap: same spot. I twisted the screws on the sight with a penny. It was a pellet gun, and I didn't want to miss. If I were shooting a varmint with a shotgun, I'd be more than close enough, but I can't shoot a shotgun in town. I had no real firepower here. Accuracy would be all.

Russell continued the story. He had hunted with a friend until about ninety seconds before sunset, when all hunting would, by law, stop, and they were more or less packing up when a group of seven wood ducks appeared in the sky.

"Man, they were moving fast; they were screaming down," said Russell, moving his hands like a little kid imagining fighter jets. He got his gun up and shot. "I dropped one into some really heavy covert. Wild rose or something."

Hazel was on the bird quickly, diving in and bashing through the water clotted with threatening thicket.

"We put the boat back in; I didn't want Hazel to drown. It can happen. They just get trapped. Hazel was working. Her nose was out of the water. I could barely see her, but I thought she had something in her mouth."

Russell turned, talking to the dog instead of me: "You got that duck, didn't you, girl! Got your first duck." Hazel did that thing dogs do when they put their two front feet out in front of them and gleefully supplicate, waiting for you to throw a stick or feed them a snack or make a move that says, "It's time to play." She took a few turns and leaps, wagged her tail, and went back to her seminap.

Thwap. I couldn't help but notice that Hazel had judged this particular gun to be of no interest to her at all. If I'd been holding a twenty gauge, she'd have been wired and ready. She was lolling around behind me, scratching her back on the grass.

Russell had called me when he bagged the duck, and I'd suggested that he hang it. I'll go out on a sturdy limb and say that what happens to feathered game when hung is not dissimilar to what happens to aging meat. Here is food scientist Harold McGee on the subject in his book *On Food and Cooking*:

> Like cheese and wine, meat benefits from a certain period of "aging," or slow chemical change, before it is consumed. Its flavor improves and it gets more tender. Exactly what happens during aging is not known, but the general impression is that the muscles' own enzymes are the principal agents. As lactic acid accumulates in the tissue after slaughter, it begins to break down the walls of the lysosomes, the cell bodies that store protein-attacking enzymes. As a result, these enzymes, whose normal function is to digest proteins in a controlled way for use by the cells, are liberated and attack the cell proteins indiscriminately. Flavor changes are probably the result of the degradation of proteins into individual amino acids, which generally have a strong flavor.

So Hazel's first duck had hung under the eaves for a few days, in feather and with the guts still in, taking on some of what the English call "high" flavor.

Russell showed me the bird, plucked and ready, and I said she was smaller than I thought she'd be. I deal with big domestic ducks most of the time, ducks bred to have breasts as big as Canada Geese. This was a little bird, like a narrow Cornish hen. Russell pretended to be hurt, or maybe he meant it. She smelled perfect: clean but gamey.

What do you want to do with her? I asked.

"I figured we'd eat her tomorrow—maybe a little cook's lunch?"

I was flattered.

"Hey, listen," said Russell, "I'm just happy to have someone to do this with. I don't always know how to eat these things. I know how to shoot them."

THE "COOK'S LUNCH" was going to be a big deal. Russell was coming over during the day to help me prep—my wife had just turned forty, and I was pulling out the stops to celebrate.

But first, I had to try to kill whatever had eaten Pepper. The anger of Achilles will not be put on the back burner while one tends to the hors d'oeuvres. Revenge is demanding.

I talked to friends about this. I called my father. He told me stories of dashing naked out into the woods in the middle of the night, swinging a rake at a possum that had been breaking into the henhouse. A friend of mine who had started the year with twenty hens and was down to five told me stories of indiscriminately blasting holes into the walls of barns, shooting at phantom raccoons with a rabid fury. It drives you to the edge.

I sat up late in my little writing shed behind the house. The window was open and the air was cool and I had a good, clear shot at the point of entry to the coop. I managed to sit there for a couple of hours with the rifle at the ready on my lap. Nothing came. Karen was locked safely away elsewhere. Around one in the morning, I drank a glass of whiskey and headed off to bed.

The next day, I watched Karen wander the yard and eat bugs. It was a sad scene, her scratching around by herself. I'm sure she missed her little society. She had no one to cluck to, no beaks competing for juicy worms. Chickens don't desire solitude. Solitude is for apex predators. Bald eagles want to be alone, peering out into the distance. If you're a chicken or an anchovy or something like that, you want to bolster the odds of your survival by standing next to lots of cousins. Watch guinea hens walk around together in a field, clustered together, and you can see their plan: when the fox runs by and grabs one of them, most of them will be okay.

People started rolling in, as expected, around three in the afternoon. We were popping bottles of champagne and shucking oysters as fast as we could. The kids were running around on the grass, playing hard and landing in big piles. The smoker was chuffing fragrant woodsmoke into the air. I'd dusted that wood duck with good salt and fennel pollen and drizzled her with olive oil. She sat in the smoker, a moderate wood fire going in the firebox, next to a rolled pork loin shot through with garlic and rosemary— basic dinner fare for when we were all hungry later. Some of us would fill up on the treats I'd bought for Rachael's party, but there are always a few who won't dive into raw oysters.

When the duck was cooked, I gave one of the legs to West, and Russell and I shared the other. I took the breasts off the bone and sliced the meat into thin slivers. She was marvelous. Gamey, high, just right. Rich with kidney flavor and blood, a wild thing brought to a cutting board. She'd had five acorns in her gullet when Russell brought her down. Russell and I smeared pâté on chunks of crusty bread and laid thin slices of the breast on top. I made one for Rachael that stopped her in her tracks and made her swoon.

That night wound down slowly, with a few late guests sitting around in our microbarn (it's set up as a speakeasy, or a grown-up clubhouse, adorned with skulls and paperbacks and memorabilia; we call it Kansas City). We were using an old chicken box—a wooden dowelled one used to transfer chickens—as a coffee table. Inside it, Karen was clucking contentedly. It was a funny way to spend an evening, but I figured if I kept Karen in a coop inside a building, she'd be safe.

I worked on her shattered home over the next week or so, doubling the wire on the walls and thinking about running some wire underground. This way, a digging animal would hit the wire and stop trying to tunnel in.

In a slow, burning fury, I sat up nights with the air rifle. I never saw anything.

While I worked on the coop, I made Karen a real cage in the barn. I felt that at least she was safe for now. I was wrong.

Rachael was out of town, and I popped up in bed, startled awake. I went downstairs, checking that the doors were locked and looking for whatever had fallen or broken—the typical middle-of-the-night security wander. I couldn't find anything. Maybe the wind had blown a trash can over. Standing over the sink drinking a glass of water, I heard a noise in Kansas City. I looked out the window. The rock that wedged the double door shut—

thirty-five pounds of granite—had been moved. The door was blowing in the wind.

I grasped at the hope, briefly, that the wind was the culprit. It was blowing hard off the river. Maybe it had pushed the door open.

Then I heard Karen warble and moan, a sound more emotive than anything I'd heard since I moved a wild rabbit I'd rescued in the woods as a kid. I picked him up to clean his cage, and he let rip with the famed cry of the rabbit, the crux of *Watership Down*. That sounds like a baby being tortured. This sounded weirder. The long, low wailing cluck that came out of Karen sounded like she knew it was the end and that the end hurt a great deal.

I was frozen and panicked. I called my wife. *What do I do? Do I go in there? She's already lost.*

First Rachael tried to convince me that since she wasn't home, I couldn't afford to go outside and fight wild animals in the middle of the night, especially since I didn't even know what it was. West needed his dad.

I claimed, hotly, that the thing wasn't going to kill me. Even as I spoke the words, I entertained a vision of a coyote leaping from the shadows to tear off a piece of my arm on the way out the door.

Her next point was inarguable. Karen was dead, or mortally wounded. If she was wounded, I was going to have to kill her.

"You're in your pajamas. If you chase it away, it'll be back later."

I had to let it run its course. The battle was lost.

I stood, hating myself, trembling at the window, waiting for something to happen.

There was a thump and another warbling moan.

I am listening to my pet being eaten alive.

I stood there for half an hour, or two minutes, or all night. I don't know. Then I saw a little hand grab at the door, which was flapping back and forth in the wind. I saw him poke his nose out and dash furtively across the yard and over a fence. A raccoon. He was huge.

My mouth opened as if to yell, but if any sound came out, I didn't hear it.

The next day I cleaned Karen up, mopped up the blood, disgusted with myself, with the whole thing, still seething at the raccoon.

He didn't leave. He kept breaking into Kansas City, looking for chickens, knocking over the tub of feed that was in there. I sat up nights. He had a pattern. I knew his path, and I had deaths to avenge.

He stopped in the yard one night, and I raised my gun, but I couldn't shoot before he sidestepped into the shadows, and I was barely sane enough to know that shooting into shadows is exactly how you end up on a neighbor's doorstep trying to explain why you shot her cat.

One afternoon, West was upstairs playing after school and I was in the kitchen. Glancing out into the yard, I saw him there, pawing at the piece of ground that smelled like Karen, because it was where I swept out the straw and blood. The size of a basset hound, he compulsively fondled the grass. I opened the door and looked at him. He stared right back, evidently fearless. There's a basket of balls by the door—West's toys for the yard. I threw a baseball at him and missed; he didn't flinch. I threw a basketball and hit him. He ran at me, thought better of it, and perched behind a chair, watching me from ten feet away. I wouldn't say he was hiding. We were making eye contact. He just needed to put something in between us. Eventually he left, but he was in no hurry.

I walked along the route he took through my yard and found, in between the house and the deck, a rather large pile of raccoon shit. He was engaged in psychological warfare. He knew we were at war. I smeared peanut butter on some paving stones in a well-lit spot and waited through the darkest hours, watching. He stopped there one night. I quietly opened the door of my writing shed and raised the rifle to my eye. He didn't even look. I sighted him in and pulled the trigger. He fell sideways and snarled. I'd gotten him! I was thrilled. But he didn't die. He ran away.

I shot him three more times. I have never hated anything the way I hated that raccoon.

Finally, we took away everything that might be interesting to eat, and he stopped coming around. I can only hope that he died of lead poisoning and that it hurt. I promised that if he came back in the spring, I would find a way to kill him. I had lurid fantasies in which I trapped him and threw the trap in the river.*

This is what it came to. I wanted chickens, and now I raged and seethed and fantasized about killing an animal that was simply doing what he does. I don't fault Russell for shooting ducks, and I surely can't fault a raccoon for eating chickens. I'm sure my well-fed Karen was delicious. The raccoon did nothing wrong, but I would kill him in a second. That's my half of the bargain, after all. It's just as natural for me to defend as it is for him to attack.

ALTHOUGH MANY of the numbers must be guessed at, a quick calculation of how much the eggs cost me is use-

---

*I've seen smaller raccoons since, but rarely. I don't think he has come back.

ful. I bought a $200 coop at a yard sale and watched it fall apart. The coop that replaced it was built with scrap lumber, with chicken wire and hinges from Home Depot. Looking around my yard, I see that I purchased a summer watering can and a heated fount for the winter. There's a feeder and a big galvanized tub and scoop for the feed. There's a heat lamp with a bulb. Repeat purchases were straw, cedar, and feed. Over the course of three years, the total cost hits about $435. I also spent a couple hundred dollars hiring high school kids to watch the Girls while we were out of town, which brings it up to about $635. It adds up to about $4 a week. Some weeks I got more than a dozen eggs, and some weeks I got far fewer. Where I live, I can buy very good eggs—real eggs from hens that roam freely on a family farm about fifty miles away—for under three bucks. I don't get the joy of watching my chickens peck at my yard, nor do I face the sorrows of their deaths. I do buy the pleasure of knowing that I am helping a farm near me stay viable.

I can't help but hope that my story puts those who are unprepared for the ordeal of having chickens off of the idea. I watch with alarm as American families put cute coops in their backyards. Chickens are the new knitting— a trend that implies domesticity and wholesomeness. But making scarves and carrying the remains of animals around are two very different things. The trend reached a pinnacle (one hopes it was the pinnacle, anyway) when Peggy Orenstein wrote an article for the *New York Times* in March 2010. It was titled "The Femivore's Dilemma" and was accompanied by a photo of an attractive woman in a well-gardened backyard. She wore muted, earthy blue and was draped with a shawl. She cradled one of her flock in her arms. She was like the California Virgin Mary, surrounded by climbing pink roses. I could only wonder how she would handle the morning she finds her chicken ripped apart with its brain sucked out of its skull. Bringing livestock home is hard stuff.

CHAPTER THREE

The King of All Cheeses

I LOVED MY CHICKENS. Having them was wonderful and elevating, and they gave us delicious eggs. Losing them threw me into a funk. Figuring out a way to buy a steer was a tremendous solution—or looked as if it would be—to a looming problem in my daily life. But cheese . . . let me tell you some stories about what cheese means to me:

In late 2010, I received a remarkable e-mail from the New York representative of Rémy Martin asking if I would like to come to Cognac and have a small tour, spend a couple of days drinking cognac, and try the crown jewel of Remy, the Louis XIII.

Rachael, look at this. Of course it's impossible; we're busy . . .

I went on to list half a dozen utterly pedestrian reasons I couldn't get on a jet to France to drink insanely expensive cognac in situ. She looked at me as if I were mad and told me to tell them yes, of course, and thank you. I'm sure I resisted. I didn't feel that I deserved such a spectacular opportunity, I guess, or I felt guilty inconveniencing others and disrupting my family life.

I have friends who are writers and high-profile spirits

people who fly around the world sipping rare elixirs and coming back with crazy stories to tell. Sometimes I envy their yarns of nights spent at castles and ice hotels. But it's not my life. For France, where I'd never been, I made an exception.

Most of my time would not be my own, but I'd have a day to recover from jet lag and wander around Paris and then another afternoon, also in Paris, on my way back. I looked at maps and made a list of things I'd like to do. I wanted to stroll through the Luxembourg Gardens, walk the streets, and stand in front of Shakespeare and Company—things I should have done when I was twenty.

I stayed at the lovely Hotel Banke, which was at one time a bank and had the marble lobby to prove it. The rest of the hotel was dark and modern, very sleek and very clean. My room was a study in black lacquer. I napped fitfully and took a shower. I was a few short blocks from the department store to end all department stores: the Galeries Lafayette. I'd peek in the huge art nouveau palace of fashion, but my real interest lay in the more architecturally modest building next door to it: the Grande Epicerie.

I was dizzily overwhelmed, practically stoned, walking through the market, gawking at the oysters and charcuteries. I was looking for the cheese counter. It was the real reason I'd come. I don't mean to the store—I mean to France. When I found it, I paced around, looking things over, wondering at the incredible precision with which the cheeses were arranged, the immense care that had been taken to present them. There were families dining on oysters nearby, and the big room was bright and lively. I found what I wanted. Nestled in the counter was a nut-orange disk, my holy grail: raw-milk Epoisses.

Une Époisses, s'il vous plaît.

The woman behind the counter looked at me sideways. She wore a lab coat and a hairnet.

"Don't travel," she said. "Risky."

I smiled. *Oui, d'accord.*

That was the point. There is Epoisses in America, but not *raw*-milk Epoisses. The Epoisses I'd had, in other words, was like that 3 percent beer they sell in Utah, or pizza at the airport—a far cry from the real thing.

I'd been dreaming of a real, raw-milk Epoisses for fourteen years.

When I moved to New York in 1996, I lived near the Fairway at 130th Street, one of the city's great supermarkets. I'd walk down a steep hill and cross the street by the Cotton Club (which had moved and has moved again), where the gospel would seep through the windows on Sunday morning. The elevated train tracks rose up in grand steel arches over what was, at that time, still a meat-packing district. There was a tiny diner right behind Fairway, buzzing with flies, where the packers would eat their dinners as I ate a cheap breakfast of an egg on a roll with plenty of hot sauce. There's a special atmosphere in a place like that, a place where two days intersect—the end of one person's day and the beginning of another's. Down under the tracks, the guys in white aprons would be smoking and eating meatloaf, winding down and getting ready to go home.

I used to go to the 3rd Street Diner in Richmond with all the other restaurant people who had gotten off work after last call and spent all night dancing and drinking beer at the after-hours club. We'd go in for crab cakes and a last round, the end of our day, while other folks sipped coffee and sat in front of pancakes, beginning theirs. There's a weird magical tension to a spot like that, as if the universe were slightly bent.

Fairway was a revelation. No, Fairway was a revolution. There, I bought excellent bagels and coffee, joints of wild boar, wings of skate, monkfish tails, and in season, they'd get boxes of chanterelles and morels. I'd never seen anything like the cheese counter there. I made a conscious decision to educate myself about cheese. I moved through the offerings—an indulgent program of study—and ate a different cheese every week. I didn't take notes, although I should have, but I was schooling myself on the deep variations, the intense craft of what bacteria, acid, and mold can do to milk. Cheese is as close to alchemy as we get. (Or it's a photo finish between cheese, charcuterie, and whiskey. I wouldn't want to have to decide which process is closer to magic.)

On the weekends, I'd put together my cheese plates— a little log of Selles-sur-Cher goat cheese, a Morbier, and a Saint Marcellin. Manchego and cave-aged Gouda and a Pecorino. I read Steven Jenkins's *Cheese Primer* and delighted in his expansive knowledge and granular detail. Consider the expertise implicit in his instruction on how to buy Morbier:

> The interior should be a nice healthy-looking, almost glossy yellowish-ivory color. The horizontal dark line of ash separating the halves should be bold and evident. If it isn't, the cheese is probably one of the several Morbier impostors—not overtly bad, just bland. Try to read the top label, although it may be obscured by age or it may be missing. If you see the label, look for a Franche-Comté/ Jura or Doubs origin and the fact that it was made from raw milk (*au lait cru*). Morbier made in factories in the

Auvergne and even Poitou is trucked to Franche-Comté to age in caves where it is shamelessly labeled Morbier. Close inspection of the cheese's label will reveal this.

Cheese was expensive, but you didn't need much. (And in fact, it hadn't gone through the roof yet. A decade later we'd be seeing prices of twenty-five dollars a pound, but back then, the prices still topped out at about fifteen dollars a pound. I could blow my mind, and Rachael's, with an after-dinner wedge of cheese that cost three bucks.)

I forged friendships around cheese: Robert Messenger, for instance—the tallest man I know and the best editor I've ever had. We've always had lots to talk about, but mostly, in those days, we talked about cheese. I'd give him a Livarot one night after dinner. He'd counter with a Colston Bassett Stilton from Neal's Yard in London.

"This has got to be one of the five best cheeses in the world," one of us would say, playing into a running gag we had about Jenkins's book in which it seemed to us that perhaps a dozen or more cheeses were thusly lauded.

I met a fabulous old matron who lived in one of the serious Park Avenue apartment buildings. (I think there are four of them, and they denote like nothing else the Waspy New York of butlers and the button on the floor to summon the help to the table.) She took a shine to me and Rachael.

"Max!" she'd say in her crazy Mid-Atlantic English, the Anglophilic accent of screwball comedies, Exeter, and champagne, which can only be achieved by tilting your head back, tensing your neck, and channeling every fiber of your Chanel suit. "I get the feeling you just don't give a damn. You do whatever you want, don't you? I love it!"

The matron would ply us with champagne, and we'd

look at her art (she had an impressive collection of draw-ings), and we'd talk about food, mostly cheese. "What's your favorite restaurant in New York, Max?"

Katz's Deli, I answered, waggling my eyebrows like Groucho Marx and wearing threadbare trousers and my one good tie.

And she'd titter with delight and launch into a story about eating at Picholine (famous for its cheese cart).

It's a shame, I said one evening over a glass of Calva-dos, *that there are so many cheeses we can't get.*

"Oh, well, I bring them in myself, you see," she explained. "I buy all the cheese I want, and I put it in the bottom of my suitcase. My suitcase has a false bottom! I had it installed. I put all the good cheese under it, and then I pile some cheese on top of it. Just whatever. So if they search my bag, they find the cheese and confiscate it. They think they've found it all, but they haven't! Ha!" She hit that *Ha!* with a great rush of breath and leaned slightly toward me. "I'm going to Paris next month. I'll bring us back some Camembert."

I came home once and found a message on my answer-ing machine; it was the matron at the top of her lungs, as if one needed to yell to get the sound through the wires of the New York telephone system, which perhaps one once had to do. I like to imagine that when she called someone, she still used the old New York prefixes, that she had a special line to an operator who sat at a desk in the base-ment of her building waiting for the dozen people upstairs who had never direct dialed a telephone.

"MOnument 5468, please."

"Right away, ma'am."

"Max," she cried into my machine, "I have cheese!" and that was it.

Her suitcase subterfuge was hardly necessary.

At the time, the cheesemongers played fast and loose with the FDA. One could stand in front of the Camembert on the counter at any of the good cheesemongers and say something coy like, "Do you have any, um, Camembert?"

Maybe they'd dart their eyes around the room, a quick head check to see if there was a guy with an official FDA Windbreaker and a radio earpiece, I guess. Then they'd reach under the counter and produce a lovely cheese that had been smuggled in for them. There were distributors who would simply send over what they knew the shop wanted, regardless of what had been ordered. So the bill of sale would say pasteurized, but the container would be full of the real stuff.

But I'd never gotten to the Epoisses. My learning curve collided with a crackdown. In 2002, a couple of kids in the town of Époisses died. It was initially reported that they had been poisoned by listeria in the cheese. This turned out not to be the case—they'd drunk pasteurized milk tainted with listeria—but it was too late: the news was on the wire. The FDA tightened up, and all the secret cheeses vanished.

So I was very happy, in Paris, to have an Epoisses. I didn't get to eat it right away. I had a short list, including a long walk to Brasserie Lipp, where I sat by myself and ate a dozen oysters (big flat Belons that tasted like the salty froth of the surf) and a tripe sausage called andouillette. I drank a glass of beer and watched as two exceedingly drunk old Frenchmen tore a hole in the bar's supply of brandy. They were trying to make fun of me and failing, disproving in one swift blow not one but two famous myths about the French—that they don't get drunk and that they are good at derision.

Back in my room, I had to rush to dinner. Then we were off on a whirlwind junket. My Epoisses was tucked away in my bag getting stinkier. I barely stopped moving for three days as we were zipped from tasting room to lunch to vineyards to dinner to the distillery to the warehouses. Back at the Hotel Banke when it was all over, having spent another wonderful afternoon walking alone in Paris, I was packing for my early morning departure when I realized that I still had the Epoisses. It was perhaps ten o'clock at night, and I sat down in front of the black lacquered coffee table with a coffee spoon and a little Opinel knife I'd bought for Rachael, which I was simply going to slip into the side pocket of my bag and hope that no one at the airport noticed. (It made it through, at least in part because I am a light packer. When I approached security with my small suitcase and briefcase, the two guys working asked where my luggage was. *C'est ça*, I shrugged. "More people should pack like you!" They smiled as they waved me through.)

The Epoisses was majestic. Runny and soft and weeping, its rind was the color of a chanterelle, with deeper striations that were like the saffron robes of a Buddhist monk. It filled the room with a heady aroma immediately—an all-encompassing sharp stink that transfixed me. The redolence was synesthetic; it waved in the air before me, bending the light in the room like heat off asphalt. I weaved before it like a hypnotized cobra. I ate. There were earth tones and deep woodland flavors. It tasted of mushrooms and barnyards and sweet, nutty butter. I understood why Brillat-Savarin—whose 1825 book *The Physiology of Taste* is to food writing as Gogol's "Overcoat" is to Russian literature, and who wrote that "a meal without some cheese is like a beautiful woman with one eye"—had called it the king of all cheeses. The power, the complexity, the levels and depth of flavor—it was a magic spell of a cheese, an utterly successful alchemy of mold and bacteria and milk.

Cheese was also a big part of my foundational food experiences. In 1980 my parents and I left the comfy suburbs of Washington DC for the rural backwoods of the Shenandoah Valley, and food became my family's First Thing.

We drove out to the country, and I remember hovering between the seats, rapt and excited as we cruised south on Route 11 and took a left onto a curving country blacktop. Laurel and big oaks clogged with caterpillar tents hugged the shoulders and J. B. Hunt trailers were parked by the side of the road. The black Angus cattle chewing cud in the fields swung their heavy heads our way to watch us pass by. Were we really listening to Waylon and Willie? It's the soundtrack I remember: "Mammas don't let your babies grow up to be cowboys . . ." I looked out across a pasture and saw a romantic, idealized vision, my own *Sheaves of Wheat*.

Our yellow house was beyond the workable, arable river basin, tucked into the tight, leafy hillbilly mountains. It smelled of mildew and hard well water. We had a wood stove and wolf spiders.

Across the road, the bank of the Shenandoah was shaley and offered up good rocks for skipping, though the sharp edges would cut into your feet if you weren't wearing shoes. The river was shallow and slow, with little bubbling rapids about fifty yards downstream. There was a hole near the far bank where the water was over my head and stayed ten degrees cooler. If I had enough fish on my string or if the day got too hot, I'd set my rod down on the bank and plunge into the swimming hole, sending the water bugs skittering.

The low, pillowy mountain behind our house was a paradise of lichens and tree fungus, and the air was redolent with the smell of humus and deadfall. One could walk in the woods for hours, and I did. The property backed up on the George Washington National Forest. I walked the ridge, followed the paths the deer had worn, listening to the cries of the red-tailed hawks above and watching the buzzards turn and bank, riding thermals and looking for carrion. With a knife in the pocket of my dirty jeans, I'd search for milk snakes and take in the views from the ridge. Except for the occasional sign indicating that the land was posted, and a particularly out-of-place tangle of long-ignored barbed wire fencing left behind by moonshiners, there was little evidence of human presence.

In our exile, we turned to food. A friend of the family started a squab farm on the Eastern Shore of Maryland, and we sold his squab in Washington DC. We also sourced the fertile Shenandoah Valley for good small-farmed lamb, beef, and rabbit. No one had invented the terms *farm to table* or *locavore*, and Slow Food was still but a glimmer in an Italian communist's monocle, but that was what we were up to.

We had been gastro-hobbyists, and we became professionals. Food became what I knew, my link to the world.

When Daniel Boulud moved to Washington DC in the early 1980s, he was not yet thirty years old, and he didn't have his Michelin stars, his television show, or a culinary empire. He had, as I recall, a Renault LeCar. Then again, it seemed all the young Frenchmen drove LeCars. Maybe it was just one LeCar that they all shared. I remember exactly the mechanism that lifted the front seat forward, rocking the whole thing into the dash with a clumsy lurch. I remember balancing a tray of chocolate truffles in one hand, leaning on the upturned seat for balance, and walking them into a restaurant with Daniel. Daniel had come to town to cook for the supranational organization known as the European Commission. He landed, as all young immigré cooks did, in the kitchen of Francis Layrle at the residence of the French ambassador on Kalorama Road, in Washington.

Francis was a key customer of my parents' food business, and he became a good friend. He'd come out to the country—I remember riding in the back of our pickup truck, sitting on an inner tube, trying to teach a friend of mine to say *FROHN-cease*. I was proud of the foreignness and the glamorous people he brought with him, with their shining watches and their little bikinis. In DC, we lounged and ate and talked in the basement kitchen. Francis would ring upstairs for more espressos to be sent down on the dumbwaiter, more little glasses of port.

His kitchen was my summer camp. For a few years, I spent summer weeks living in his bungalow and spending time with his friends. He had a pool, and we'd play pétanque, and I'd have a great time walking around the city and learning the bus routes, going to the National Gallery, and coming home to wedges of Morbier and Camembert. In the embassy kitchen, I squeezed pastry bags and piped the fillings into miniature tarts and stood next to his charming prep cook, Marie Elena, trying to trim batons of carrots with a paring knife.

My parents' business expanded when Daniel went home to France to visit his mother, who had a farm outside of Lyons. When he returned, he brought with him real rennet, the milk-digesting enzymes from a young calf's stomach.

Traditional rennet is derived from the inner mucosa of what is called the "abomasum," the fourth stomach, of young calves. The enzymes are there to help coagulate and digest their mother's milk. The received wisdom is that cheese was discovered, or invented, depending upon how you look at it, by people who stored milk in such tied-off stomachs and carried it with them. When they opened their primitive canteens, they found whey and curds, which can be quickly manipulated into rudimentary cheese. They must have been hungry to even try it. (Kudos to all those first movers, though. Can you imagine staring down an artichoke and deciding that there was a way to eat it?)

To harvest rennet, the stomachs of young calves slaughtered for veal are cleaned and dried and soaked, usually in salt water or whey. The enzymes dissolve into the soaking water, which is poured off and is now usable rennet. Daniel stuck some of it in his luggage and brought it home to my mom. Shortly thereafter, she started making chèvre and became the Cheese Lady.

Smuggled rennet was only the beginning of the Cheese Lady's malfeasance, however. It was—and still is—illegal for farmers to sell raw milk. It was also illegal for her to take that milk and turn it into cheese and sell it. It's not as if we invited the health inspector around, installed an all-stainless system of sinks with super-hot water, or dedicated a commercial refrigerator to milk and cheese storage. We found a farmer willing to play along, and we drove the mountain roads, two-lane blacktops, through the George Washington National Forest past Elizabeth Furnace, where Passage Creek had once powered a blast furnace to process iron ore mined nearby into pig iron, which would float down the Shenandoah River to Harpers

Ferry to be forged. (One of the great idiosyncrasies of the Shenandoah Valley is that the river flows north, so "down" is up.) The goat farm was nestled in the woods, a little hollow swarming with animals. There's an old picture of me in a pile of hay, having been playfully tackled by a dozen goats now intent on eating my sweater. We'd drive off with five-gallon buckets of raw, whole milk. Sometimes just a couple, sometimes half a dozen, occasionally more.

I'd carry the heavy buckets down the shallow stairs from the driveway. The house had started as a little mountain cabin, and the living area was one big room onto which we'd added bedrooms on either side. A thick Boos butcher block, six feet long, divided that central area, and everything on one side of it was kitchen. The house, looking back on it, was mostly kitchen. I'd set the buckets up on that butcher block, and Mom (and sometimes me) would add a teaspoon of rennet and eight tablespoons of buttermilk to each bucket. After a couple of hours, the milk would have curdled into solids and whey, and we'd slice them on a grid and spoon the slick, tofu-like blocks out with a shallow ladle drilled with holes. Then we'd drain the curds in cheesecloth suspended over another bucket. There was no time frame for the drying of the curds. A strict time frame would have only annoyed my mom even if it had been justified, but in this case it would have been impossible. The water content of the milk changes with the seasons and the condition, age, and activity of the goats.

When my mom deemed the curds dry enough, usually after a couple of hours, we'd put them back on the butcher block and blend them with salt in the KitchenAid stand mixer. The cheese, at this point, was done. My mom's chèvre was fresh and wet. I've since learned that most chèvre is, in fact, acidulated—cultured with bacteria instead of coagulated with rennet. Hers remains the best I've ever had.

And there was nothing like it on the East Coast in 1981. We'd pack it into white five-pound containers and drive it into the city: foodie bootleggers.

MAKING CHEESE can be very easy. If you've ever curdled milk in lemony tea, you've already done it. Actually, if you've ever left milk too long in the fridge and watched chunky, solidified goop go down the drain, you're already experienced with the process. Neither of these things tastes good, though, and good is what we're after. (Laboring under the anxiety of Mom's influence, I was after more than good. When I called her to ask for a refresher on how to make cheese, she answered as if I were a seven-year-old doing math homework at the kitchen table, asking for help with easy addition. "Why don't you tell me?" *Seriously, Mom?* "You know the answer; just think about it for a second and then tell me how to make cheese." I gave it a shot, running through the process as well as I could remember. I got close. "You forgot the buttermilk," she quipped. I tried to stay calm.)

Let's start with the basics. Cow's milk is 87 percent water. The remaining 13 percent breaks down as follows: 0.7 percent minerals, 3.5 percent protein, 3.9 percent fat. The last 4.9 percent is a sugar called lactose, which proves interesting. According to food-chemistry expert Harold McGee's *On Food and Cooking*, lactose is found in three places: the flowers of forsythias, a few tropical shrubs, and the breasts of mammals. (The first two produce little of it.) Lactose is a multiunit sugar—one glucose molecule and one galactose molecule—and to be used by the body, it must be broken down by the digestive enzyme lactase, which is found in the small intestine. We have a lot of lactase when we are born, and then our bodies slow down its production. By the time we're about three and a half, we don't make much of it. Most mammals don't drink milk at all after they are weaned and therefore don't waste resources producing an enzyme to digest it. If a sugar makes it through the small intestine and into the colon, it can ferment, producing carbon dioxide. Sugar in the colon can also cause water retention. The sugars in milk, in other words, make most of the people in the world gassy and bloated—sometimes harmfully so. Lactose intolerance isn't the exception; it's pretty much the state of things. Here's the good news: people of Northern European descent generally produce enough lactase to digest milk. Here's the even better news: in fermented dairy, like cheese and yogurt, the bacteria that cultured the milk used the lactose as fuel. They've already digested it for you. There is barely any lactose in cheese. (There are, it seems, people who are allergic to the proteins in milk, but that is something else altogether.)

There are a lot of different proteins in cow's milk, but for our purposes we need only deal with two of them: whey proteins and casein. Casein is a little collection of components bound together into something called a micelle. The micelles have a negative charge, making them repel each other, which keeps them evenly distributed throughout the milk. When acid or the enzyme rennin is introduced to the milk, the charge is lowered, and the casein micelles clump together to form curds. The whey proteins, meanwhile, remain suspended in the water. The milk has thus been separated into solid curds and liquid whey.

To make cheese, one introduces the proper bacteria

and enzymes to milk, and the milk ferments. The miracle of fermentation means that the beneficial and flavorful bacteria outpace the pathogenic ones, preserving the milk and creating layers of complex flavors.

Layers of complex flavors—well, that's the rub, isn't it?

I didn't want to go through the entire process of making cheese to end up with farmer cheese or some rough chunk suitable for keeping huns alive as they rode to the next great plunder. I wanted some refinement.

Rachael saw an advertisement in one of those magazines you find by the door of the health-food store. Hawthorne Valley Farm was offering cheese-making workshops, and they were doing one on Camembert.

They were offering four hours of hands-on instruction at the dairy with the cheese maker who works at the farm, and promised some discussion of raw milk and raw-milk politics. I signed up.

I drove an hour and a half north on the Taconic Parkway. It was a beautiful spring day, the trees still in pale green, everything on the come in late April. Hawthorne Valley Farm is about ten minutes east of the Taconic, straddling pastoral County Road 21C. Within moments of my arrival, I was texting Rachael to announce our imminent move.

On the east side of the road is the Hawthorne Valley Waldorf School, which teaches K through twelfth grade. The campus is woodsy, with a stream that cuts behind the nicely arrayed buildings. There are tetherball poles and basketball courts and a theater and classrooms.

On the west side of the road is the farm. Three hundred and sixty acres of mixed-use biodynamic land, strictly in line with the teachings of Rudolf Steiner. (This means, among other things, that they think that cattle are connected to the cosmos through their horns and that the staff walk the farm during the winter solstice burning incense.) They make sauerkraut, bake bread, garden, and keep a herd of sixty dairy cows. They do a fair amount of teaching in the educational center on the farm. The store there is among the best I've ever seen. They've got excellent coffee, fantastic bread, a great counter of cheeses not limited to their own, a cooler of raw milk, and biodynamic yogurt. When I first stopped in, there were two pretty farm girls in muddy boots and dirty Carhartt dungarees leaning against the wall and drinking kombucha. Hawthorne Valley Farm delivers. It's what upstate New York is supposed to be like. I fell in love.

The creamery is built into a barn, back behind the education center, past the sauerkraut cellar. (Fermentation everywhere! The smells wafting out of that cellar were intense. Their sauerkraut is magical.)

I stepped into the anteroom to find Peter Kindel before a motley assortment of about twenty-five students, young and old, knowledgeable and newbie. There were two or three couples, one of which was vacationing in the area. There seemed to be a few regulars who'd blurt out, "Oh, like in the other class!" Peter would nod and say, "That's right, Mary."

Peter is a bright, unnervingly fit man of about forty years. He stood in knee-high Wellingtons and a snug gray t-shirt, and he looks as if he should be racing bicycles: light, strong, sinewy, defined. I kept playing a little movie in my imagination in which he took off his outer layer of clothing to reveal cycling gear, hopped on a racing bike, and pumped into the peloton of a passing race as he smiled his good-byes. Before we went into the creamery and began the class, he gave us a rundown of his history. About twenty years ago, he'd looked at his wife and asked why they couldn't get any good cheese. (This is the sort of thing people say, and it suits the American tendency to imagine ourselves an uncultured herd of rubes. It's not true. Murray's Cheese, a truly excellent shop, has been open in New York since 1940. A franchise called the Cheese Shop had about ninety stores in America in 1960, a hundred years after the first one opened. There has always been some good cheese. There's more now.) He'd been to France where, it goes almost without saying, quality cheese is a part of the culture. Over the next two decades, he rang all the bells, a whirlwind of perfect cheese experiences. He went back to France. He worked in Vermont. He worked in New York City at Picholine and at Murray's. He helped open the restaurant Artisanal (which has its own cheese cave). He moved to California and made cheese there. Someone asked him what the most expensive cheese in the world is, and we learned that he'd made a crottin that won best of show in a contest and was subsequently auctioned off for around $800 a pound.

"Maybe that?" he said with a playful grin. I wondered if the question had been a setup—maybe the person who asked it was a regular and played the part of a shill to steer Peter into his best material.

He's a very happy man. When a parade of cows passed by the window, milkers moving down a path to a barn, he stopped and we all watched.

"It's so nice to see them."

About three years ago, his wife put in an application for their child to go to the Waldorf School at Hawthorne Valley, and in a brilliant stroke of luck, the farm told them that their cheese maker/creamery manager was leaving and asked if he would like the job.

Indeed he would.

When he arrived, he shook things up by changing the line of cheeses they were making and started producing his favorite: clothbound cheddar. It's a brilliant cheese with a nutty, salty depth.

The creamery itself is wonderfully clean. It smells tart and sharp and sweet, like an ice-cream shop, with an undertone of things washed constantly with hot water and steam. We stood around a stainless-steel table, and he showed us how to culture and curdle the cow's milk. He'd started some the previous night, and we saw how the disks would shrink in the molds. We salted them and turned them. When the curds had a clean break—you lift them with a thin spatula and they break in a straight, clean line, as if sliced—we cut them, let them sit for a little while longer, and then spooned the curds and whey into new molds.

Over the course of a few hours, he did what all good teachers do: he made a daunting process seem plausible. Then we ate cheese and asked questions.

Within days I had everything I needed. From the New England Cheesemaking Supply company I ordered molds, the bacteria, *Penicillium candidum*, and rennet. I bought a new stainless-steel bain-marie pot. (Please, he implored us, don't use the stockpot. You'll never get all the animal bacteria out, and it will make truly funky cheese.) I bought a reasonably priced wine chiller that would hold at fifty-four degrees—the perfect temperature for aging cheese.

You need to have a five-hour stretch of time to make Camembert. You won't need to attend to it during that time, and in fact, each step takes only a moment, but you need to be available. You are on call at the cheese production facility, as it were. At five in the evening, I gathered my equipment, put a big pot of water on to boil, and washed my hands fastidiously. I looked over the recipe and double-checked that I had everything I needed—molds, molds, enzymes, bain-marie, bamboo mats, plastic containers, whisk, ladle. Check. I sterilized everything with hot water and then lowered the water in the big pot to just below a simmer. I poured a gallon of Hawthorne Valley's lovely, sweet, butter-yellow raw milk into the stainless-steel bain-marie and held it in the bigger pot for twenty seconds at a time. Then I'd take the milk out of the bath, give it a gentle stir with the ladle, and take the temperature. It was at eighty-eight degrees Fahrenheit in no time—forty-five seconds or a minute, tops. (Instant-reading infrared thermometer guns have gotten cheap—you can still spend hundreds of dollars on one, but mine was twenty dollars, and it reads up to one thousand degrees. It's perfect for milk, deep-fry oil, barbecue, and shooting at your friends to see how hot they are. West likes it because it looks like a ray gun and shoots a red laser dot. So I guess it *is* a ray gun.)

I put the milk on the table and sprinkled in one-eighth teaspoon of mesophilic starter (a suite of bacteria called MM101 in the cheese-making catalogues) and a pinch of *Penicillium candidum*. I waited for five minutes as the cultures rehydrated on the surface before I stirred them into the milk using a whisk. You stir milk up and down when making cheese because a liquid stirred with an up-and-down motion has no leftover momentum—it doesn't keep going after you stop. If you stir around and around, as one usually does, the milk starts to set while the milk is still spinning, and the curds form along the vortex in the whirlpool. I'm not sure why this is bad, and

I'm tempted to try it just to see it happen. But this was my first shot at Camembert, so I did as I was told.

The starter bacteria, which begin reproducing immediately, serve a few functions. First, they outpace and eradicate whatever weak pathogenic bacteria are present. Good bacteria are stronger than bad bacteria—that's why plants that are not vibrant are at risk for blights, and that's why, to put it plainly, we're not all dead from the many, many pathogens we encounter daily. The bacteria also begin to acidify the milk and begin the curdle. All cheese-making bacteria perform the previous functions, but different bacteria impart different aromas to the cheese. The *Penicillium candidum* (also called *Penicillium camemberti*)—one of many *Penicillium* molds and not efficacious as an antibiotic—is a fungus. It forms the white bloom on the rind of the cheese because it grows in the presence of air. (It doesn't, in other words, grow inside the cheese.) The *Penicillium* grows on the exposed surface, and its enzymes work on the inside of the cheese to change the molecular structure. Over time, the cheese will ripen, and the enzymes of the *Penicillium* will change the bland, chalky interior to a creamy, smooth, unctuous, and almost liquid one. But I'm getting ahead of myself; the ripening comes last.

I set a timer and let the starter culture sit in the milk for two hours, checking the temperature occasionally. I would hold the milk in the water bath to warm it when necessary. I tried to keep the milk between ninety-two and eighty-four degrees. The mass of the milk and the stainless steel it was in did a pretty good job of holding the temperature. I only had to fine-tune it to keep it on course. A moment in the bath and a quick stir did the job.

When two hours had passed, I added one milliliter of

rennet, which I'd diluted in nonchlorinated water. As in almost all processes during which we manipulate the tiny organisms of the world to make things taste good—baking, gardening, brewing, cheese making—the chlorine in our water works against us. (Make no mistake: I'm glad the chlorine is in there. I've seen the reservoir where my water comes from, and it's clear to me that possums and deer and various fauna are constantly shitting in it.) Rennet will begin curdling the milk right away, and it is important to leave it alone until you get a clean break. It *should* take about forty-five minutes, but there's a lot at play, and you have to let the curds tell you when they are ready, not the other way around. Cut into the curds and lift up. If the curds cleave without crumbles and don't cling, you've got it. The curds should open up, with a good, defined edge, and will be smooth, like soft tofu.*

If something goes wrong, chuck it. After all, you are working with a controlled rot. If the spoiling doesn't happen the way it should, then maybe it's truly spoiled, not artfully spoiled. Mine came like clockwork, and I cut the curds into one-inch squares, crosshatching with my cake spatula, and let them sit for another forty-five minutes to shrink a little. I ladled curds and whey both into the 4.5-by-4.5-inch cylindrical forms, which are dotted with drilled holes to let the moisture escape out of the side. I'd placed the forms on a bamboo sushi mat on top of a cooling rack in a roasting pan. The roasting pan is key, because the whey will drain. My gallon of milk filled four molds, and they were noticeably draining within a quar-

---

*A clean break, like an elephant, pornography, or good architecture, is hard to describe. Don't round up or down, don't rush it, don't fudge. Trust yourself. You'll know it when you see it.

ter hour. When they were halfway down, I flipped them over by putting a second bamboo mat on a second cooling rack and awkwardly flipping the whole stack. The more you flip cheese as it drains, the better looking it will be. Since it had to drain overnight, it was eventually left on its own to settle.

The next morning, my curds were disks. I was astonished. I could pick them up and hold them gently, which I did to salt them. I used roughly a teaspoon of flaky, noniodized salt per disk. I went so far as to roll the edges through a dish of salt. The salt will season the cheese and dehydrate its surface, which is the first step in making a rind. My bamboo mat was wet with whey, and I soaked a thin plank of wood in filtered water and put it in my cheese-aging fridge to keep the humidity up. The cheese went into the fridge and sat there, looking amazingly like cheese. Within a few days, the rind had started to bloom white and puffy, and things were starting to smell less like curdled milk and more like cheese—richer, fattier, nuttier. I flipped and tended the cheeses. One of them got stuck on the mat and the rind tore off, which was disappointing (the humidity had dropped, I think, but I also suspect that plastic needlework mesh might be better suited to the process, as it would be naturally less grabby) but revealed what was going on underneath. Sure enough, there was a layer of creamy, smooth Camembert. I licked my finger and was amazed: my disks were on their way. About 80 percent of the bloom grew back in two days. When the cheeses looked like they really had a rind—a solid covering of mold—I wrapped them in parchment and put them in a Rubbermaid container to ripen. It was up to the *Penicillium*, now, to turn my dense little pucks gooey and flavorful over the next three weeks.

One afternoon, as I was picking up at the Glynwood CSA, the blue-eyed all-American cutie-pie volunteer there indicated that they'd started to get some cheese in, and we could buy it from the fridge.

West piped up immediately, bless him: "My dad is making cheese!"

The girl's face lit up, and she exclaimed, in a rush of breath, "Really!"

Now, I must admit a weakness for making blue-eyed hippy girls smile. (It wasn't something I'd recognized until that very moment. I came home and told Rachael, who smiled and squinted her own blue eyes and had one of those terrific moments available only to wives, I think, or maybe wives and good editors, where you've suggested something about yourself as a surprising revelation that has long been obvious to them. Of course Rachael knows; that's why we're married, after all.) If a blue-eyed girl of the sort who volunteers to weed carrots smiles at me, I'm off. So I was all information and big smiles, right away. But sadly, I didn't have anything all that good to report.

I'm trying, I said. *My little disks of Camembert are hard as rocks, though. I think I'm losing too much whey in the molding, or the humidity in my aging fridge isn't high enough. It works*—this is the moment at which I'd gone on too long, by the way, but she was still paying attention—*I mean, it smells right, and I can even taste how it is headed in the right direction, and I get a good bloom from the* Penicillium, *and that enzymatic action should be working on the cheese, but it won't get gooey.*

"Do you have animals?"

Shit—why don't I have animals? I thought.

I've been getting raw milk from Hawthorne Valley, I said.

That actually seemed to work. She was psyched.

"We can't get it to curdle," she said.

Huh?

"I guess we didn't use enough vinegar or something . . ."

I launched into a small thesis about how she should really use starter bacteria and how if she used raw milk—she did—it was pretty risky to simply try to acidulate the milk to curds with vinegar.

Raw milk doesn't want to sit out on the counter overnight. At all.

The truth must be told: I put my failure into dialogue because it makes me sad, and I don't like confronting it directly. I'd made eight disks of potential Camembert, and most of them were crumbly, puck-like, and dry. I had snapped a disk in my hands the day before, broke it in half as if it were a thin sheet of dusty rock, which, in fact, is exactly how it crumbled. I chewed a piece, dry as Romano, and I got some nice cheesy flavors, but it was tough going—lots of licking of the teeth and masticating and swallowing and trying to get rid of it.

One disk (the thickest of the first batch) appeared to be right. I smelled it and pressed it in my hand. It seemed like what I'd meant it to be. I resolved to take it to my parents' house for my father's seventieth birthday. You know that whole thing when you go to someone's house for dinner and they're all like, "Oh my, I've never cooked this before; I hope you like it! This is an experiment"? Yeah, well, here I was, playing the oldest trick in the book but upping the stakes.

We ate it our first night there. My dad put out a splendid board of charcuterie. There was cured beef from Spain, a salami, and a rough country pâté of duck he'd made himself. He'd pickled some onions and beets, and we also had small, sweet, and briny Turkish pickles. There, on the wood next to all these delights, sat my little disk. It looked lovely and right. It looked like it belonged.

I was trying to pretend that I wasn't as nervous as a sixteen-year-old at a driving test as my mom cut a wedge out of the disk and delivered it to Dad's plate (first dibs to the birthday boy, after all).

It was cheese. Pops was generous and said that it was my own thing.

"It's a hands-on process that speaks of the maker," he said. "You've made *your* cheese."

I hoped this didn't turn out to be true. It was too salty by far, too sharp, and too gummy—like a cold Brie with a thickening agent. It had an aggressive tang that you'd call "sharp" if it were a cheddar. I can't say that it was entirely bad, but it wasn't entirely good.

This cheese was too dry and not fatty enough. More humidity, I decided. Less salt, obviously. Less draining.

My mom asked if I knew the fat content of the milk I was using. I didn't. As much as I loved Hawthorne Valley, maybe I needed to find someone who milked Jerseys, or any one of a number of breeds known for their high fat production. I had gotten close, and I was too far along to let it get me down. I'd made cheese, after all: now it was about making the right cheese.

CHAPTER FOUR

Dakota

P ERHAPS THE MOST NATURAL and self-evident way to get closer to the food you eat—the meat you eat, anyway—is to hunt it yourself.* I've been toying with the idea of hunting for years. It takes time; it takes prep; it takes dedication. I wanted to see what it was like to find food in its wild state and kill it myself. Russell has hunted birds for most of his life, and he talked enthusiastically about his yearly trip to North Dakota to shoot the wild pheasants there.

The words *pheasant hunting in North Dakota* ring out in a special way. When Russell talked about the trip, which he'd been going on for a decade before I hitched my wagon to his train, I envisioned two-inch-thick buffalo steaks and one of those big stone fireplaces burning five-

---

*There has been a little flood of books, recently, which would tend to indicate that I am not alone in this conclusion. Most of them are good; some of them, like Steven Rinella's *Meat Eater*, are flat out excellent. It's not just a popular subject, however; the number of hunters has risen steadily over the past few years after many years of decline, and it seems that those who come to hunting now are likely to be cosmopolitan, hip, farm market folks.

foot logs. I figured we were headed toward a lodge: heavy timber, good rugs, big leather chairs, the heads of dead things decorating the walls.

North Dakota is the deep end of the pool. That was good with me. I wasn't interested in the shallows.

I've done a fair amount of walking in the woods with guns. I've strolled around on a sunny December morning loaded for deer, but never with any real intent. The hunting I'd done had been social, Southern. It typically ended on the lawn with a fried turkey, some barbecue, some beer.

I'd never been on a hunting trip.

I found that I was less than halfway ready. I began to prepare in earnest. Absurdly, my idea of preparing for a hunting trip was to read the Spanish philosopher Ortega y Gasset's treatise on hunting.

For while there was shopping to be done—manic shopping, really; one could wear a credit card out getting ready to go hunting—it wasn't what concerned me the most. What concerned me was the killing. (Hence, my reading of philosophical treatises.)

This wouldn't be a possum in the henhouse. It wasn't the raccoon I'd so desperately wanted to shoot. This time, I was the one on the prowl. I was the aggressor. I was going out looking for things to shoot at, hoping that I could knock a bird on the wing out of the sky.

As a kid, I used to walk down our dirt road to play at a once-a-farm where my friends kept a Saint Bernard who would put you right on the ground by way of greeting, his big paws on your shoulders and his huge tongue licking your face. Theirs was the barn in which I shot my first pigeon: a sad affair. My friend and I tried to gang up on a barn pigeon with a brace of pellet guns, and he fell but lived. He was weak and at our feet, and we didn't want to kill him any longer—I don't think I'd ever wanted to kill him, really; I'd only wanted to shoot at something. We had to plug him ten, fifteen, thirty-five times with pellets before he finally died. It was wretched work, and neither of us was smart enough to simply pick up the bird and wring its neck—we were too young, too green, and we didn't know what to do with a bird that we'd knocked down but hadn't killed. I was mortified.

Those who have grown up hunting accept this transaction automatically, which is not to say that they are unmoved. Even the most seasoned hunters confront the death of their quarry with religiosity and gravity. Years ago, I took a hunter safety class in New York, because there was no way to prove that I had taken hours upon hours of instruction as a kid in the Shenandoah Valley, where hunter safety was a solid part of our school's curriculum. (From the tone with which it was taught, I gathered that this class was the most important thing we studied. Other things were taught because that's what gets taught. We learned geometry because it was time to learn geometry. Hunter safety was on another level, and it felt odd that it was delivered with such earnestness, but in retrospect, they were right. Like driver's ed, this was a class during which the instructors were very directly trying to teach you not to kill anyone, or yourself, with your own adolescent inattention or impetuousness, both of which they saw constant evidence of.)

Years later, there I was again, now in my thirties, sitting criss-cross applesauce on the ground with thirteen-year-olds, listening to the lessons about how one must keep the barrel of a gun pointed away from one's compatriots at all times. I learned that I should keep a small ration of food I don't like when I walk into the woods so I won't snack on it and be left without sustenance when things go wrong. (If you filled your pockets up with Snickers bars, they pointed out, you'd simply eat them when you got bored.) They told stories about putting animals out of their misery, about finishing the job. They guaranteed that we would wound an animal and find ourselves having to deliver the final blow. And they told us to get ready, because it wasn't going to feel good. But it would be too late. You would have already made the deal; you would have already pulled the trigger. There'd be no going back. The whole thing is terrifying, if you stop to think about it. And you should stop to think. And you should be frightened.

Russell and I did sneak in a little nearby hunting. The weekend following the opening weekend for pheasant, we slipped out of our houses in the predawn and hopped in his truck. Hazel—his Brittany spaniel—was in the backseat. Russell had long told me stories of her psychic powers: "She *knows*, man. If I even think of hunting, she's at my feet. If I'm sleeping, dreaming of hunting, I'll wake up and she'll be right there." (I did, once, point out that perhaps he was dreaming of hunting precisely because his dog was panting nearby, a reversal of causality of which he didn't seem to want much.)

This morning at 4:30, closer to the time I like to go to bed than the time I like to wake up, she certainly didn't seem like she knew what we were up to. She was thoroughly unimpressed, lolling in the backseat of Russell's four-door Tundra with her chin draped over her paws.

The sun rose as we cruised the highway, and I noted that we were not the only truck on the road with a dog crate in the bed. (It was too cold for Hazel to ride there now, but later, when she was muddy and tired and the sun was out, she'd relish the refuge of her little fortress.) We were headed to a place called the Great Swamp, which is stocked with pheasants by the state of New York. When we exited the highway, Hazel stood. She spent the rest of the drive climbing into the front seat, scrabbling over the center console, nose up, looking through the windshield. She did know.

She knew so much, in fact, that when we started missing turns and driving in circles, her disgust was palpable.

"See? She knows. She's thinking, *You missed the turn, asshole.*"

I couldn't deny it. (And later, in fact, I'd have more of this sort of interaction with Hazel. A hunting dog expects things of the hunter, it turns out. Knowing the way to the spot is only one item on the list.) Perhaps she could smell the birds?

I was . . . not nervous, exactly. Nerved up, certainly. Questions were looming large. A maxim of intelligent hunting is "Know before you go." I knew nothing. Could I do this? I hadn't even been to the trap range yet—this hunt had been impromptu, an all-of-a-sudden decision motivated by the fact that my new shotgun had arrived. I'd never shot it. I wasn't nervous about that, though. Guns are guns. I'd be used to this one in no time. I was nervous that I'd find myself torn asunder by the immediacy of having really intended to kill something and having followed through.

I had given this much thought, of course. I had been reflecting on hunting and had worked through the logic: I kill things all the time—just not with my own hands. If I'm okay with eating meat, then I need to be okay with killing, because killing by proxy and leaving the wet work to someone else is bullshit; it's lying to yourself. That's allowing yourself to be seduced and hoodwinked by the slick cover we've laid across what is a gigantic culture of death—a constant grinding death machine that is ending the lives of animals at a staggering pace. But just because I'd worked through the logic of the thing didn't mean I wouldn't find myself heartbroken, sad, and guilty in the early morning sun.

What if I simply didn't want to shoot? It had happened before.

BECAUSE MY CHILDHOOD HOME was on the hill and the hill faced north, we built our garden on a stretch of flat ground—the only bit that got any sun. It was a good garden: my folks had dug some railroad ties into the ground, and we had slightly elevated segments for different types of plants. Zucchini overgrew one rectangle, and tomato cages were spiked in another. We had melons, lettuces, and all manner of domestic flora that would tempt a groundhog out of its burrow and onto the surface for a nibble—a relatively harmless example of what happens when man interrupts the habitat of beasts with something delicious.

We didn't take kindly to it, however. Groundhogs could and would eat your garden down to dirt. High summer was punctuated by groundhog vigils.

I sat one afternoon on our porch next to my father; I must have been eleven. I was of the age when my tenderness toward animals was at its height, topped only perhaps by my desire for approval from Dad.

He wore a wide-brimmed straw hat. His .22 Remington rifle leaned against the porch railing. I'd shot it plenty, but I was much more interested in keeping things alive than I was in killing. My rabbit, the cats, the dog, even the Rhode Island Reds laying eggs over to the east side of the house—I loved them all.

It must have been a hundred degrees. It was heaven— except for the gnats that came at us like clouds.

"I'm going to go inside and get a drink. You watch for groundhogs."

I was thrilled. At eleven, being told that you are in charge of all you see (I was up a hill, on a porch, looking out over a river valley) and that you can rule it with a loaded gun—well, that's about as good as it gets. Better than driving the car.

I looked at the rifle, and I looked at my dad, and I looked at the small field below, and I nodded.

He took his time.

Sure enough, what comes along but a vegetable-eating brown ball of fat and fur: a groundhog.

I looked back to the sliding glass door through which my father had disappeared, I looked at the gun, and I looked at the brown fur waddling across the lower acre.

I picked up the rifle. It had a push safety on the trigger guard, and I pushed it so that the red part of the column showed. It was a semiautomatic with ten shots in the magazine. I'd shot this gun a hundred times or more, so it was familiar in my hands.

The thing is, at this age, I was a very good shot. I'd proven it over and over again shooting at targets in the yard, shooting black-powder rifles at the Belle Grove Plantation Fair, and shooting my BB gun at action figures and coffee cans.

I got a bead on the groundhog.

My focus was astonishing. I was no longer seventy-five

or a hundred yards away from the animal; through my sights, the animal might as well have been sitting in my lap.

I breathed.

Careful breathing is an important aspect of shooting well.

He was wobbling toward the zucchini.

My father was not coming back. The responsibility had fallen on me. I was looking down the barrel of a gun, and I had a good shot on this varmint that was shuffling around in our vegetable garden, a varmint I was supposed to kill.

I wanted to kill a groundhog for Pops.

I watched the groundhog, and I saw every roll of fat as he stepped; I saw the dull glint of his eye sucking in the light. This thing on the other end of my barrel was alive.

Despite the glory that would have come, I couldn't shoot him.

My father opened the door, and the noise startled the groundhog away. I don't even remember if Pops noticed that I'd been pointing the gun at something.

THE GREAT SWAMP that Russell and I worked that morning is about 444 acres of land. Some of it is meadow, and some of it indeed feels like a swamp. When we got down into the wetlands, where the marsh grasses and the cattails grew over our hats and we had to push our way through the thicket while our boots sunk into the mud, I kept hearing the opening riff of Creedence Clearwater Revival's "Run through the Jungle" in my head. I almost expected Russell to turn around and mime instructions to me, pointing and gesturing as if we were characters in a movie about a war in a wet, tropical Asian wilderness. In the swamp, I couldn't imagine how we'd get a shot off—I couldn't see past my hands. Hazel was out there in the reeds; we could hear her, but we had no real access to her.

Later, we walked a flat field with strips of thigh-high covert. Hazel bounded in front of us, zigzagging across an imaginary square that was restricted on all sides by the range of our guns. Imagine a sort of goalie box, limited on either side by Russell and me, who were walking with perhaps twenty yards between us. Hazel would go ahead then loop back as if to check in. She would leap through the tall grass in front of Russell and then across the box and in front of me. She was consuming air, smelling everything she could, looking for birds. It's an amazing thing to watch, and one learns very quickly what dogs are for.

It was opening day of the New York season for waterfowl, and in the distance we heard the steady crack of shotgun blasts, but we saw no birds. We saw occasional piles of feathers—there had been birds, but there weren't any now. They'd been hit hard by hawks and coyotes. (Hunters don't leave dewy, matted piles of feathers behind—that's the work of something's teeth.)

Walking back toward where we'd come in, across a scrubby high meadow, we weren't quite sure if we were done for the day. (It's hard to give up on hunting if you haven't shot anything.) A lone hunter stood by the side of a windbreak at the edge of the field, looking bored. I was closer to him, and as I got within speaking distance, he asked if we'd seen any birds. He had his gun on his shoulder, and I told him we hadn't—only some feathers and remnants. He had theories about the schedule the state used to stock the fields and when hunts might be more successful, and we wondered together about how long a bird let loose would stay in a given area.

Russell was moving along to my right with Hazel in

front of him. Suddenly, there came a great rustling, and I turned to see Hazel flushing a bird. It wasn't a pheasant.

Time slowed. I saw Russell shoulder his gun in slow motion; I saw the bird leap into the air, pausing about five feet off the ground, getting its wings going. Russell took a shot, and the bird started to move; he took another, and the bird flew past him.

It was a woodcock.

I felt bad for not having been actively hunting—I'd have had a shot at that bird if I'd been where I was supposed to be, rather than shooting the breeze with some stranger.

Russell was visibly disappointed, more for having missed his first shot of the year than in me. I didn't need his disapproval, however. I felt like a fool. If I'd been on the job, we'd have had a woodcock to eat.

We drove back home and found Rachael and West still in their pajamas, just starting to cook breakfast.

I learned some lessons that morning. The first was small but vital: I needed some brush pants. My legs were soaked and cold, scratched by briars and thickets. The real lesson, however, was that I needed to pay attention and stay in the game. That woodcock should have been mine.

I decided that I should get used to the new gun and practice my shot. I found, conveniently, that the Blue Mountain Sportsman Center in Westchester County was only fifteen or twenty minutes south of my house and had ranges for skeet and trap, as well as rifles and handguns. It was an odd revelation that so much was so close. If you didn't know or you weren't interested, you would drive right by the parking area for the Great Swamp without giving it a second thought, and I'd never have thought there would be a county-sponsored shooting range so close to my home. I wondered if this was what it felt like to be a Mason, to have a world revealed to you that was there all along, invisible only because you didn't have the key to the code.

Blue Mountain is down a little two-lane road, past rock walls and old suburban country houses interspersed with bigger, crummier houses that had been built as the original owners subdivided their generous lots. It must have been a great place once, the kind of suburb in which Cary Grant and Katharine Hepburn might chase around a leopard.

The drive felt familiar, although I couldn't imagine why. By the time I walked up the steps to the little wood-paneled lodge that serves as the office, I was giggling to myself.

This is nuts, I said as I walked in. The girl behind the counter must have thought I was talking about her. She bristled and asked why. She had a couple of rings through her lips and must have confronted the puzzled and bemused expressions of NRA members and cops all day long. I explained that I had taken my hunter safety exam almost a decade ago in this very lodge.

I handed her fourteen dollars and drove through the woods, past the archery range, to the skeet and trap center. It was a drizzly fall day, and the two guys who run the place—retired policemen—were smoking cigarettes in their little shed.

"Trap or skeet?" they called to me.

I said I didn't know; I'd never done this before.

"Trap."

They proceeded to coach me, becoming more and more interested as the shots rang out.

"I'm gonna duct-tape your head to the stock of that gun if you keep looking up like that."

"Might be kinda hard for him to drive like that . . ."

"Stop jerking the gun. You're jerking it!"

I shot very badly but then better, and their enthusiasm came right along with mine.

I turned around and said that it felt really good when the clay breaks, and they shook their heads in faux dismay.

"You're done for."

"I came out here twenty-five years ago, never had done it. I'm still here."

"You'll be here in twenty-five years. I'll be in a wheelchair over there, and you'll say that I'm the one who got you started!"

It does feel amazing when the clays break. It's a release in the same way that a perfect golf swing is. You're not thinking about it; you just do it, and then, smoothly, without conscious effort, everything slips right into place and the little orange disk that is whipping away from you shatters gracefully.

I telephoned Russell with my newfound enthusiasm.

"Yeah," he said with a shrug I could feel through the phone, "just wait until something dies."

It was a hard reminder of exactly what it was that I was preparing myself to do.

There's a great bit of country wisdom expressed in the phrase "That's why they call it hunting, not killing." Hunting is the whole act, the chase, and what's more, it isn't necessarily successful. Even a hunt that is, in fact, successful, will have hours of trudging through rough terrain, missed opportunities, missed shots, and no game. You can sit in a hunting stand for a week and not see a deer. Killing happens at the abattoir. Killing, even at its most basic—let's say the slaughter of a single chicken for a Sunday dinner—is orchestrated. You walk into the pen, choose the chicken, grab it, and chop off its head. Killing is what happens when a flat of soft-shell crabs shows up, and you have to process them. Killing is throwing a bunch of lobsters in a pot.

Walking in the woods with a gun is not the same, because the outcome is unknown. If you are holding a bag full of lobsters and boiling water, there is only one way the story is going to end. While hunting, things aren't so perspicuous. You might see something to shoot, you might not.

That said, killing is the point. If you keep trying, the hunt will end in death.

If you hunt and you have never considered whether or not killing is okay, you are missing some key element of humanity. I should be clear here: I'm not saying it is necessary to be troubled by it. I'm only saying that it is necessary to think it through. No one should take death for granted.

I considered it at length.

Much has changed since I pointed a rifle at a ground-hog. I've butchered. I've cooked. I have carried whole lambs with their heads still attached into the backs of restaurants. A whole lamb has an eyeball-popping look that will spook you until you finally grow accustomed to it. The wool sets the living lamb's eyes in their heads, but when skinned, they look . . . well, they look like Marty Feldman. They seem surprised in a gruesome, bloody way. I've skinned deer. I can deal with meat, in other words. I was sure, in fact, that once the animal was dead, I'd be fine. At that point, it's meat. Even guts—they aren't gross; they're just delicious or not delicious, depending on which bit they are. Even offal I don't particularly like—chicken livers, for instance, are too ferric tasting for me—I can still handle and treat well. But the key moment lay in front of me. The moment of transition. The turning from animal to meat. The moment of death.

I had wanted to discover how I felt about shooting an animal before I flew all the way to North Dakota. I didn't want to stand there after hours of flight time and travel and realize that I wasn't interested in killing things.

Then it looked, suddenly, like it might not be an issue.

Through a series of miscommunications and cancellations, the whole hunt was almost called off. I won't bore you, or myself, with the details of what had gone wrong, but I will say that I had to scramble to pull it off and that I found myself at Newark Airport with a dog in a crate (having never flown with a dog) and not only my own gun (ditto about flying with guns) but Russell's as well.

I took Hazel out of her crate and tried to get her to pee, but she was too excited. Russell was right. She knew that if she was traveling in a box she'd be hunting soon. She lunged at the lead on the sidewalk in front of the terminal, desperate to start. She would have run off looking for birds in the long-term parking if I hadn't been gripping her hard, scared of losing her, scared of calling Russell with the news that I'd lost her or that she'd jumped under the wheels of a passing Lincoln. (That she might, in fact, give up the ghost on the plane and I'd arrive with a dead dog was something that we'd talked about—something he promised not to blame on me, although I didn't believe him.)

MOST OF THE PARTY came together at the airport in Bismarck. Jimmy Hitchmough met us there, already in full field dress. He'd brought a feisty young Brittany spaniel with black maps, Velvet, up from Maryland. Hitchmough, at this point of the visit, maintained a sort of Delmarva good-old-boy charm. He was a weather- and whiskey-beaten sixty-odd-year-old, a friend of Russell's family from Maryland. Dick Gordon, a friend from back in the Hudson Valley, had flown out as well. We got the keys for our rented SUVs, walked the dogs, and drove across the flatland while the sun set. The prairie stretched out on either side of the highway, and it still looked blank to me. Magnificent in its sweep, I hadn't gotten to know it yet. From a car window, a prairie is an expanse of khaki brown, smooth as an ice-skating pond.

We stopped in Dickinson for supplies. We bought shells at the Walmart (a sentence that brought no small amount of amusement to the wives back home—"You're what? You're buying ammo at Walmart?"). We stopped at the local butcher for thick steaks and pounds of good bacon. The liquor store where we laid in whiskey had more taxidermied animals on display than anywhere I'd been save Cabela's or the Buckhorn Exchange restaurant in Denver, Colorado. We drove on a grid—no turns for miles—in the way that one can drive only in the western states. Soon, we were flying down gravel roads, kicking up clouds of dust in our wake.

It was dawning on me, as I saw the spare landscape and the plain farmhouses, that perhaps we were not, in fact, headed to some glorious lodge with rich carpeting and a huge fireplace.

Indeed, the house into which we unpacked our stuff was utilitarian. Kids had grown up here. The television received only Fox News, Fox Business, ESPN, and the Outdoor Channel (what more would a North Dakota hunter need, after all?). There was brick-colored shag carpet and an old, worn electric stove. From the basement wafted unfortunate odors. It had been confirmed the previous year, during an investigation toward the source of the smell, that the sewage line leading out of the house was at least a little bit open. We chose our rooms, opened beers, and unlocked gun cases.

This wasn't the Filson catalogue version of manliness. This wasn't Teddy Roosevelt. There were no stuffed bears, no zebra hide, no fireplace. Even the wine glasses we found in the cabinet looked out of place: Who drinks wine out here?

We headed into the tiny town of Regent for a saloon dinner of griddled steaks and iceberg. Everyone was in brush pants and blaze orange. Aside from the bartender, I don't think there was a woman in the place. Men sat at tables of six and eight with their hats on, talking quietly. I had expected some camaraderie, but there was none to be had. Weren't we all here to do the same thing? Weren't we, one and all, here with our dogs and our guns? No doubt, if I'd run into any of these men in the bank or the airport, and we'd seen one another in brush pants and orange, we'd have talked for forty-five minutes. The lines in the Cannonball Saloon, however, were not to be crossed. Guys would walk by, dead eyeing their way to the bar without a nod or a tip of the hat. Were they protecting their territory? Had they all failed to find any birds? There was music on the juke; there was a card game in the corner—things should have been gregarious: back-slapping, dirty jokes, and hunting stories. We chewed our steaks and drove back to our Jack Daniel's.

I went to bed with a strange mix of anticipation and anticipatory disappointment.

Was this all worth it? I'd flown halfway across the country, lugging guns and dogs, to sit in a sullen room and chew through a crummy steak?

We were all up early the next day, just before dawn, and we stood around the kitchen, slurping coffee and eating egg sandwiches. Russell outlined a plan: We'd start at a spot called the Bull Pasture, where there was a stretch of covert (called a shelterbelt in Dakota)—some trees that jutted off a road on a right angle. Dick and Russell would bring the dogs up to the end of it and walk toward Hitchmough and me, who would be stationed in a ditch.

I put twenty-five shells into the loops of my hunting vest, grabbed my Browning Silver Hunter twelve gauge, and eased into Hitchmough's little rented Dodge. We listened to the Blue Collar Comedy station on the satellite radio and found common ground over our mutual appreciation of Ron White.

Everything I can say about North Dakota will fail to deliver the magnitude. It was windy. Not blustery. Not forceful in the way that those of us who are accustomed to a steady kite-flying wind off the ocean understand it. It was just a solid rush of wind without restraint, without peaks or valleys—just wind like a radio tuned in between stations: solid, white wind. I tucked down into the grass in the ditch; the ground was cold, but it didn't penetrate the way the wind did. So I dug in, and I waited.

I heard Russell calling out to Hazel and Velvet off in the distance. They were working, and I was waiting. I didn't see anything. Nothing was happening.

Then I saw a bird; it looked like a hen (off-limits in North Dakota), and she was flying in the wrong direction, too far away, but it was a bird. Then another. Then a dozen. Then there were birds pouring out of the side of the woods, all flying off into a field to the right of the shelterbelt, away from us and out of range, but on the wing and numerous.

I could hear the dogs now, crashing through the brush. I could hear Russell talking to them. There were birds on the wing. *Hundreds* of them. And as Russell and Dick moved closer with the dogs, the birds moved closer, too. They were breaking toward me now, moving into range. A big rooster broke out of the woods and flew across, headed toward eight o'clock. It was a thirty-yard shot. I lifted the gun, got my eyes on him, slapped the trigger, and down he came.

First shot, first morning, first hunt.

I couldn't believe it. I tried to gather my thoughts—birds were everywhere. I took two shots and missed, scrambled to get more shells, and missed a couple more. I was too shaken, too overwhelmed, flush with . . . what can I call it? First blood? That sounds awful.

I walked over to my bird. There were still birds in the air, and Hitchmough was taking shots. I just wanted to see what I'd done. My pheasant was big and beautiful and ever so slightly still alive. I picked him up by the head and swung him around to end it. His feathers were iridescent. Magical. I'd shot him. I'd crossed over.

I was right about the instantaneous transition: he was already "game"—no longer a bird, already simply an ingredient that I'd been lucky enough to gather for myself.

When I worked as a short-order cook, I was always troubled by the most banal orders: scrambled eggs, tuna fish sandwiches. In both of those cases, I knew that I'd be doing it worse than the customer could at home. The tuna is crap, and it's been in a bin for who knows how long. The eggs are scrambled too quickly in margarine so they won't brown, on a flattop griddle that is too hot; I can't stir them properly, and they are left to sit with their big curds hardening while I plate a round of french toast or check the cheese melting on an English muffin under the salamander broiler. I did the best I could, considering the volume and the speed required of me, but I was ashamed that I couldn't do better.

I felt no shame in my kill. Killing isn't the shameful part. This bird had lived in the wild (and in the case of a rooster pheasant, he'd done a particularly violent job of it, killing babies and spurring hens out of the nest so they'll get shot or eaten by the predator he's avoiding, eating all the food before any other birds have a chance at it) and died in the wild. In a wild way. It all felt right.

Our days in North Dakota were among the finest days I've ever passed. We laughed like hell and cooked excellent dinners, which we served with sharp knives and big glasses of whiskey. I called Rachael from the parking lot of the gas station in town, where I had some cell reception.

It's amazing. We're having so much fun. We're all just laughing and getting along and telling jokes. And we walk fifteen miles a day, I think. We're all muscle sore and tired out and loving each other.

Except for Hitchmough. He'd be blind drunk before dinner every night, pissed off that we weren't ready with his supper at 6:00 p.m. Cranky, senseless, knee-walking drunk, he'd sit in a recliner gazing into space with the television on, and then he'd get up and tell us lies and bitch, and then he'd pour himself a pint of shitty Canadian whiskey and go back to his perch in front of the TV. He was a whirlpool, a sinkhole of negativity. He was dependent upon us; we were to provide him everything. He couldn't walk, because of some problem with his knees, so it was our job to put birds in front of him. He couldn't cook, because of some problem with his soul, so it was our job to put dinner in front of him. Everything I had gone hunting to get away from, he brought along.

Shooting my first bird had felt great. In the following days, I collected two more moments that will remain in heavy rotation while I play through the mental slideshow of my life. People might wait a lifetime for both of them, and I feel lucky as hell.

The first came after a long series of fruitless walks. We'd segment our days out—we had 6,500 acres of farm to hunt, plus public land, and we'd work sections methodically. Many of these sections were big in a way I'd never experienced anywhere. Marching orders came from Russell. He'd point at a rough map of the area and say something like, "Max will walk this fence line until he sees us, and we'll walk this fence line over here, perpendicular."

They'd drop me off, and I'd walk for an hour before I saw them. Often, I'd walk watching birds jump and fly away ahead of me, well out of range. But I'd keep an eye on where they'd headed, and we'd try to surround them once we met up and send the dogs into the area and see if we could flush them out.

On these long walks I got to know the prairie. It looks uniform, but it isn't. There are winding ditches, and streams, and knobby stands of old trees. There is equipment left in the field, stranded where it broke. There are patterns of mule deer beds like miniature crop circles in the tall grass. There are three or four types of grass, and flowers, and prairie dog holes inviting you to step in them and twist your ankle.

One day had proved especially difficult. The grass we walked through was waist high, and I had to pull my

legs through it as if it were water. This went on for hours
while the wind blew and the mule deer stotted off into the
distance. There were no birds. Finally, we came to a small
meadow with short grass (small in North Dakota means
it was maybe twenty acres). We were walking together,
with the dogs running in front of us. The dogs were tired,
too, but they were on a scent and pulling on reserves of
energy because they were excited. The sun was low in the
sky, and we were almost done. The SUVs were on the road
toward which we walked, and we were looking forward
to the kitchen table and cold beer. With the sky just turning gold, Velvet went on point in front of me. The hunter
closest to the dog when she goes on point takes the lead.
It was my responsibility to walk up and flush the bird hunkered down in the grass. The first shot would be mine,
too. Hazel came up behind Velvet and backed the point,
standing sideways behind her. It was beautiful, the stuff
of hunting calendars, but in paintings it looks calm, and it
is not. A dog on point is a dog transfixed, overwhelmed
with scent, a bundle of instinctual potential energy stilled
by training. They tremble: riveted, focused, boiling. Hazel
had her front leg cocked. I walked quickly toward Velvet's
nose, looking at the grass. A bird taking cover in the grass
is invisible. It hides better than anything you can imagine.
(To point out just how invisible they can be, consider this:
One afternoon, having decided we were done for the day,
we stood by the road and talked. Four of us stood in a
circle, and I stood a few yards away, putting my camera
in the SUV or something. We stood around like that and
talked for ten or fifteen minutes, and then, from right in
between the boot toes of my friends, a big rooster pheasant leapt into the air. He got above their heads as they all

yelped in surprise. All of them raised their guns and shot straight up, and all of them missed. Russell asked me later why I hadn't shot at the bird: *Well, he was about three feet over your heads,* I said, *and I've been shooting at stuff enough today to surmise that it is not inconceivable that I'd miss something by three feet.*) Although the grass was short and the land was flat, I could not see the iridescent feathers of an animal the size of a small chicken right below my feet. I walked, kicking the grass.

The bird leapt, with a plosive pop of feathers gathering air and the distinct *chortle chortle chug chortle* that a rooster cries when taking wing. It's tremendous and startling. The bird flushes quickly and moves fast, but you're so focused that every motion it makes is clear. I saw every one of his long tail feathers as he gathered the wind to fly. I saw every movement and shudder of his wings as he flew dead away from me. I brought the gun to my cheek and fired. He fell.

"Holy shit," said Dick. "That image is burned into my memory forever; that's one of the most beautiful things I've ever seen."

I gathered my bird, and we walked toward the SUVs. Russell walked beside me.

"By the way," he said, "that was a going-away shot."

I had told him that at the range I had trouble hitting the clays that went away. Crossing shots I had figured, more or less, but I'd found it hard to judge a target flying straight. It was kind, heartfelt praise, a sprinkling of pure sugar on what was already a perfect moment.

My second peak—or third, really, although a first bird is a peak that everyone shares and doesn't really distinguish itself in any way except for the person who pulled the trigger—was far more raucous. We were working a thirty-acre plot of public land, and we were undergunned and underdogged. Russell calls it "getting Dakota-ed" when the space you are dealing with is just too big for what you've got, and you watch the birds all fly away out of range. We were walking a pattern across the field, hoping to push some birds over to the two hunters we'd stationed on the road.

The field started high and slowly slanted toward the road, with little folds and ditches and bunches of taller grass throughout. We'd been walking about ten minutes when we saw four or five big black SUVs come speeding along and stop in a cloud of dust on the edge of the field next to us. Forty hunters disembarked, a huge party, with a ton of dogs. They surrounded the big field to our right and set the dogs to working it. They were making a lot of noise, and their dogs were yipping, and we all stopped to watch them in their matching blaze vests. What happened next was pure magic. They started moving birds. First a few hundred, then maybe a thousand, and then tens of thousands. The pheasants blackened the sky above us. We shared some glances: this was lucky. We were all easily one hundred yards apart, me and Dick and Russell, in the field. We hunkered down. Wave after wave of pheasants came over us, and the shooting started. I heard balls of shot clicking together over my head—*snick snick snick*— as the lead pellets brushed against each other. Then I thought it was raining—what was falling all around me? I noticed lead bouncing off of my vest: Dick's shots were falling on me—harmless after traveling a hundred yards or more, but exciting. The birds were well on the wing, flying high and fast over our heads. I had maybe fifteen shells left from a day of fruitless shooting. I shot them all and knocked down two birds. When I ran out of shot, I nestled into a small hollow and watched the majesty of the birds flying over me. They careened, flapping in bursts and drifting this way and that. It was stunning, and I was glad that I had no more shells to shoot, that I could just let go. I lay in the grass next to my warm gun, ankles crossed, bathed in sunshine, enthralled as the birds flew.

CHAPTER FIVE

Grow Your Own

I 'VE BEEN A GARDENER for more of my life than not, though not a serious one. My parents are serious—although never fastidious—gardeners. One of the reasons they'd left the city was to raise their kid up on more peaches than television. That meant that I worked the garden. Usually my efforts would begin under duress, with the natural protestation of a boy told that he must work, and settle into enthusiasm after the first swing of the hoe, or after I got into weeding a patch or digging potatoes. Once your hands are dirty, once the first potato has been summoned from the furrow under which it's been hiding, or the first bit of earth is weed-free and left for only the plump shoots of what you will later eat, it's hard not to get zealous. Few satisfactions run as deep or have such antediluvian resonance as knowing that those tender starts are growing and thriving and might ultimately feed you.*

---

*That's why it's hard, for all but the best of gardeners, to thin seedlings. They must be thinned, of course, or they'll bunch and deprive each other of nutrients, but it's hard to plant a seed, have it grow, and then decimate the babies so that the survivors may thrive. You look at them and think "Oh! It worked!" And then you punish that success.

(And few things are as heartbreaking as when things start to go wrong.)

The short, smooth mountain on which we lived in the Shenandoah Valley faced north—our house clung to the side of it, our porch sticking out over the hill, where I'd sat and watched the groundhog—which meant that we had dazzling sunsets over the big mountain ranges to our left and that we had excellent, constant light for painting if only any of us were so inclined. This also meant that the ice at the foot of our driveway never melted and that the garden had to be as far away from the house as possible, on flat land down the hill that my folks had bordered with something like a hundred autumn olives, which created a wall of shabby privacy and a shelter from the dust of the dirt road. Autumn olives are considered an invasive species by some, and by others a resource for food. I don't remember them growing outside of their line or producing anything we'd want to eat. I just know that they formed a good covert, a line of thicket that had a pass on the northwest corner through which I could scoot if I ducked my head.

It was this garden that delivered my first great horticultural disappointment. I had fallen in love with the small pickle called a cornichon. It's nothing but a gherkin, but it's cured with champagne vinegar—extra tart, super clean—and for some reason that escapes me now, it was the best thing my twelve-year-old mind could imagine.*

My family had a thriving cottage industry by the time I thought of contributing to it with cornichons. Mom was making chèvre. We were selling rabbits and squab. Fol-

---

*I'd been heavily into pickled things since I was a baby. I would, at a tender age, open the door of the fridge and find the jar of capers and eat them with a spoon until the jar was empty.

lowing with the generosity of kids everywhere, I wanted to contribute. (I've seen it in West, who is willing to walk upstairs and break his piggy bank open to contribute funds if Rachael and I are talking about money within earshot—when asked why he won't spend his allowance on a Nerf gun he particularly wants, he answers that he wants to save his money in case we run out. I understand that he is playing me, trying to get me to buy it for him, but it's a generous instinct, I think.) My plan: to make and sell cornichons.

I commandeered a patch of ground and cultivated it, setting it up like a pea patch, with fence posts at either end and a netting of nylon string for the plants to climb. The gherkin is knobby and prickly like a kirby, but smaller. I sowed my seeds after all threat of frost had passed, and the seedlings were soon wrapping soft tendrils around the string, ready to climb. I remember that things looked good. Gherkins like shade—despite their rough appearance, they are tender plants—and they didn't have but the passing shadow of the weeping willow up the hill. Still, the plants twisted up the netting, and I got a good first blossom. I looked at them frequently, and we watered them as much as we watered anything else. It was early in the season—June, I'd guess—when I plucked about half a pint of cute fruit and brought it up the hill to the house in the fold of my shirt the way one of the girls in *Little House on the Prairie* would fill an apron.

I canned those pickles in a brine of champagne vinegar, dill, and garlic. I remember pulling the jar from a canning bath and learning about how the heat would create a vacuum that would pull the lid down hard on the jar. I remember waiting for them to be ready and looking at my little Ball jar, half full of my first experimental round of cornichons, with mustard seeds floating around and drifts of herbs all army-green drab and suspended like seaweed. It was wonderful because they looked just right.

Childhood is a series of hopes, some dashed, some rewarded. The first time you struggle into a plastic Halloween costume from the store, you are disappointed because it crinkles and tears and no matter how hard you try you don't actually become Spider-Man, with webs shooting out of your wrists and the ability to climb your living-room walls (even though you insisted that the plastic costume from the store was the one, the magic, the solution).

My test batch of cornichons was exactly what I'd wanted it to be. The gherkins on the vine, however, were not playing along. Cornichons are pickled in about three weeks, and as I neared that date I noted that my crop had not continued as it should. I got two here, three there—a small handful was all I ever managed after that first half pint.

I cracked the jar, and I knew even then that I was set up for disappointment. If they didn't taste right, I'd have failed as a cook; if they did taste right, I'd have failed as a gardener.

I remember the taste vividly. They were bright and crisp, and they snapped on your tooth in just the right way. I'd made fantastic pickles. So I settled in with mixed feelings. I'd wanted to be the king of the cornichon, but that ship was not going to come in. This was my first lesson in the unpredictability of gardening. It seems to me that it still captures the truth: gardening delivers joys and sorrows in almost equal measure.

The joys are summery, sweet, and fleeting. What can match a handful of sugar snap peas eaten off of the vine? To this day, my parents chuckle at how they'd send me down to the garden to pick peas, and I'd come back up empty-handed.

"Where are the peas?" they'd ask.

I'd explain that there hadn't been any.

They were confused for a while. They'd seen the peas that very day, after all, while tending the garden. Where had they all gone? It took a few times before I came clean and admitted that I'd eaten them all right there, standing at the trellis.

The fruits of your labor don't always bring joy, however, even if you manage to get them all the way to harvest. I remember vividly the Tragedy of the Chile Peppers.

After Rachael graduated from college in 1992, we drove from Virginia out to Yellow Springs, Ohio, our little Toyota packed with records and books and sweaters. I'd been accepted at Antioch, and I was looking forward to finally finishing college after various misadventures. We figured we'd find an apartment and find Rachael a job that suited what we thought she deserved after graduating (this is another of those Halloween-costume disappointments, of course, the bizarre idea that one is qualified for anything after marching up to get a diploma). I remember long drives in summer heat, windows down and the radio on. We'd pull into rest stops and pick up the little flyers there that advertised deals on hotels—in 1992 you could still stay in a motel for fifty dollars. We had saved up enough money to make the move—and not much more.

Upon our arrival, the disappointments came fast. The school hadn't come through on financial aid in the way I'd been led to believe it would. The apartments we looked at were dreadful. The only job listed in the paper was at a copy shop.

We tried. We stayed in a motel for a couple of nights—

still harvesting what fun we could from the trip, enjoy-
ing our diner breakfasts and cups of coffee while we
scanned the meager want ads. As we started to realize
that it wasn't going to work, we drove three hours north to
a cottage owned by Rachael's grandmother on the shore
of Lake Erie. We stayed at the cottage for a week or so,
feeling adrift and talking about what we were going to do.

We were alone. We were in a foreign land—all flat, dusty
roads and brutal, squared-off buildings that looked more
like pillbox bunkers than homes to us. We were used to filigree and southern wood. The cottage was a little box surrounded by thin grass, with a garage that housed a boat
we dared not try to use. We read and we talked. We swam
in the lake (was it our imagination or were people looking at us like we were crazy?). Our bed smelled like dust
and citronella: summer camp. We cuddled on the glider
and laughed and watched the thunderclouds roll in during
the afternoon. We drank beer, and with her grandmother's
dull, old knives, we prepped the simplest dinners I've ever
cooked.

A roadside grocery was only half a mile away. They had
faded cans on the shelves, but there was a table of bright
fresh produce from a nearby garden. We bought beer, coffee, a pint of whiskey from the shelf behind the register, a
flat of tomatoes and zucchini, onions, greens, eggs, potatoes, butter, and olive oil.

The vegetables at that roadside grocery were delicious,
especially the tomatoes. I cut thick slices of them, seasoned them, dredged them in flour, and then fried them
in olive oil until they were perfectly golden brown. We'd
eat them along with cans of beer on the porcelain-topped
kitchen table. We'd also purchased a bottle of Trappey's
Indi-Pep hot sauce. We thought it was lovely, the label all

curlicued and printed with fancy script, like something a
snake-oil salesman would sell off a wagon. It was a tiny
extravagance, and the zip it added to our repast was
exactly what we needed. We shot our over-easy eggs with
hot sauce in the morning, and we splashed it on our fried
tomatoes in the evening, and it was colorful and vibrant
and awake. Those meals will remain forever on the short
list of the best food I've ever eaten. We were making
something out of nothing. We were not buckling under,
but rather rising to the occasion. We weren't going to be
stopped. Our crispy, juicy ripe tomatoes with the vinegar zing and a little bite of chile pepper and salt were all
we needed.

We moved back East and settled in Richmond, where we
got jobs at restaurants. The following spring, we cleared
the ailanthus and the plantain weeds out of the yard and
hoed in a neat rectangular garden. We planted tomatoes,
basil, dill, a couple of squash, and, inspired by the magic
of Trappey's Indi-Pep, lots of chile peppers: long Anaheim
chiles; thick jalapeños; papery, super-hot habaneros; and
a bush of cayennes. The plants grew well in the swelter-
ing heat of that summer—it was, that year, one hundred
degrees or more every single day in May. The peppers
blossomed and the fruit arrived; weirdly, they all looked
the same. We picked them all and I began processing them
to make a huge batch of our own hot sauce. There were no
habaneros, so I seeded and stemmed and chopped without gloves.

By ten o'clock that evening I was sitting on the floor,
staring at my hands. They were on fire. The shape of
the chiles had been that of thick Anaheims, but the roulette wheel of cross-pollination had landed on the heat of
the habanero. I felt like Antoine in Jean-Paul Sartre's *Nau-*

sea, who didn't recognize his own hands. Rather than an existential disconnect, however, my disaffection from my own physicality was caused by intense, steady pain that came in relentless, pounding waves, each beat of my heart bringing a surge that broke upon the shore of my nerves. It was too much to even consider as real pain. It became an abstraction.

"Maybe we should call Poison Control," worried Rachael. She likes to laugh at other people's pain. She agrees with Mel Brooks: "The difference between comedy and tragedy is if you walk into an open sewer and die, to me it could be comedy . . . but tragedy is if I cut my finger." She wasn't laughing, however, which is always a terrible indication that I might be truly hurt. I couldn't ignore the comedy of the situation myself, even if my chuckles were those of the condemned man, a bit of gallows humor as I sat down to pee or asked Rachael to scratch the itch in my eye.

Although I shrugged off the suggestion at first, we called Poison Control at midnight. *They* thought it was funny and didn't even pretend to do anything but laugh at us. At two in the morning, I called my mom. She suggested I soak my hands in milk, which I did, and the cool fat began to calm the fires.

The Tragedy of the Chile Peppers left us wary, but we continued gardening until we moved to Manhattan, where arable land is so precious that there was a six-year waiting list for a community garden plot. I wish we'd known about grow bags back then and planted on our fire escape, even if it meant braving the wrath of the walleyed super who was quick to remind us that fire escapes were for *escaping.*

When we moved to Brooklyn, we had a backyard. I

searched the EPA website for what they call "Right to Know" alerts in my neighborhood. You can plug in a zip code to get information about toxic events—spills and anything about which you might have, as they say, a "right to know" are represented by a colorful dot on the resultant map. The map of Greenpoint that my search summoned looked as if someone had upended a trash bag full of confetti on top of it: streets were obscured, entire blocks covered with layer upon layer of dots, each of which meant that something had happened there. We dug furrows in our yard and filled them with hundreds of tulip bulbs. Spring would be colorful and fun (and I wish I'd seen the look on the next tenants' faces upon their first spring there), but it wouldn't feed us.

When we bought our little house in a Hudson Valley village, we dug in flower beds, watched the sun, and started a garden, which went well for a few years. We grew carrots and tomatoes and cucumbers and herbs, and we did it all for fun, never taking it very seriously, never turning it into work.

After all, we had the Cold Spring Farmers' Market, which is a joy. I love getting my vegetables there. It was at that farmers' market, in fact, that I began to sow the seeds of this book, thinking about how a section of America had set up a new, secular kashrut. Kashrut is the name for the system of Jewish laws that define what is kosher and what is forbidden. Aaron Bobrow-Strain wrote in his book *White Bread* that "thanks to an explosion of politically charged food writing and reporting that began in the late 1990s, members of the alternative food movement have access to a great deal of information about *why* and *how* the food system needs to change."

Concern about the country's food—where it comes from, how it is grown, what it contains, and how it affects our bodies, environment, and society—mounts every day. Stories about obesity, food safety, carbon footprints, and conditions on farms and in food factories appear daily in the media, heightening the growing sense that something is wrong with the U.S. food system. In the face of this, an energetic new social movement—often called the "alternative food movement"—has exploded onto the scene. A diverse assemblage of locavores, farmers' market lovers, community-supported agriculture subscribers, fair trade coffee sippers, New Agrarian back-to-the-landers, artisanal food enthusiasts, home cheese makers, backyard chicken raisers, community garden organizers, neo-traditionalist advocates for "eating like Great-Grandma," hardcore and occasional organic food purchasers, co-op shoppers, and Slow Food gourmets, the alternative food movement is hard to pin down.

Obviously (the evidence is in the table of contents to this book) I am most of the things that Bobrow-Strain has listed.* What I've noted about my cohort is that much of this activity (some of it painfully self-righteous) is based upon anxiety. There should be no anxiety. I can't stand the anxious eater. We should make better decisions and remedy that which requires remediation. Meals, however, and the stuff that goes into them, should be fun. The Cold Spring Farmers' Market fit that bill. In the best possible way, it felt like going to church. I cannot be alone in noting that farmers' markets happen on the weekend and in the morning. We don't quite scrub up for them the way that our fore-

---

*I also don't bristle at his little poke in the eye—make no mistake: he doesn't invoke this list as a celebration. Or, rather, he invokes this list straddling the line of derision and celebration, as he should.

bears got themselves tidy for the weekend sermon, but we do show up knowing that we'll be in public. It's a wonderful bit of community: the townspeople all gathered in the sunshine, the kids with Popsicle juice running down their hands, farmers and growers and winemakers all hawking their wares, and all of us celebrating the sun and greeting one another. It's a great Saturday morning, and aside from the occasional whiff of smug satisfaction (which only adds to the churchgoing vibe, really), the farmers' market is the simplest example of the growing movement to change the way we eat. It is, also, totally without anxiety. You're just buying excellent bread, and some mushrooms, and picking up a bunch of arugula and a ripe tomato, and checking out what kinds of pickles the women with tattoos have brought this week. The Saturday-morning market is a revolution without the anger of Luther. (I am tempted to insert a joke about the Diet of Worms, but I can't quite figure out how to do it . . .) Clearly, the growth of farmers' markets implies that I am not alone in believing that this is an excellent expression of our new attitude, and an excellent tack for where we are headed. A quick look at the numbers from a graph entitled "Number of Operating Farmers' Markets" published by the USDA shows a remarkable increase. There were 1,755 farmers' markets in 1994. The number grew steadily through the decade and then started to really jump: almost a thousand more popped up between 2009 and 2010, and the following year saw another 1,043 new markets—a 17 percent increase.

Because I love going to the market, I narrowed what I wanted from a garden to tomatoes and basil. In fact, we have extraordinary tomatoes from the Four Winds Farm in Gardiner, New York, at the market, but I love having a tomato plant in the summer. I love the smell of the leaves as you brush up against them. And I love having tomatoes warm, right off the vine. I reshaped my bed and wound a soaker hose through the plot, which I put on a timer for when we were traveling.

I chose my varietals and bought sixteen starts. I had a few San Marzanos, a few yellow tomatoes (I don't remember which), and the rest were Brandywines—a classic, almost clichéd tomato, which is pale red, juicy, and sweet. They are the only varietal that gets close to the best tomatoes I have ever had, which aren't a variety at all but more like an unofficial AOC* out of Hanover County, just north of Richmond, where the soil and the growing conditions produce what is, quite simply, the best tomato on earth. (There are lots of places that make this claim, I know. I've had others, and I've had tomatoes that get close, but I've never tasted a tomato that surpassed the ones out of Hanover. Don't argue with me; just go to the festival they have there. It's worth the trip.)

I dedicated myself to the patch, bringing more energy to the process than I ever had before. I side-dressed the tomatoes with organic fertilizer three weeks after they'd been planted, and things were looking good. Leggy, maybe, but good.

---

*Despite the immense progress made in the United States regarding the respect and understanding of our foodways, we have yet to officially recognize some foods as specific to a place. France has the appellation d'origine contrôlée (AOC) for wine and some agricultural products, while Italy has the DOC (denominazione di origine controllata). Certain things, according to their rules, must be made in a traditional manner and in a certain place to be sold with a certain name. Champagne, for instance, can't be made anywhere except the places where it has been made historically. Tennessee whiskey is one of the few American products to have received such a designation. Our Tax and Trade Bureau formalizes the appellation of some wines, but they haven't expanded it to include cheese or tomatoes.

And then . . . the details are foggy. With traumatic experiences, I've learned that one either remembers them in terrifying, slow-motion detail or not at all. This one I've suppressed as well as the events that led to me driving my big, old 1976 Caprice Classic through three hundred feet of fence line and two locust trees in 1989. I was driving to work, then I was driving through the woods, then I was standing on the road, with blood pouring out of my face. I have no idea what happened. As to the tomato plants, as best as I can remember it, everything stopped. The plants stopped growing, and the blossoms were sparse— ridiculously so. I had three blossoms where I should have had hundreds.

This was 2009, the year the *Phytophthora* blight hit the Northeast—the same blight that caused the Irish Potato Famine in the 1840s. It is something you can plan for and protect against, but it is not something you can fix once you have it. It can't be lived with. It rotted my stems and weakened my plants and left me in shambles. Margaret Tuttle McGrath of the Department of Plant Pathology and Plant-Microbe Biology at Cornell University wrote in "Late Blight: Recent Occurrences, Challenges, and Future Outlook," a paper published by the Cornell Extension Office, that "2009 was unprecedented especially in the northeastern US because late blight was very widespread, started to develop very early (June), was present on tomato plants for sale at garden centers, and had tremendous impact on growers and gardeners." Everyone got it. The CSAs were tomato-less, causing many of their customers to desert the programs. Rumors flew around like hungry bats, but the most prevalent one was that it was caused by people buying crappy tomato starts at box stores, which seemed too handy, too neat to be true. McGrath wrote that "definitive knowledge of the source of these outbreaks would be helpful for managing late blight in the future," which implies to me that they have some idea where it came from but can't prove it.

I got one tomato. I'm not even sure that I ate it, fruit of sadness that it was. I ripped out the bed, reshaped it again, put down black weed fabric and a bunch of river pebbles, and planted half a dozen coneflowers. I was done with gardening for food. I told everyone who'd listen that I'd never hoe a furrow again. I was at gardening rock bottom. Nothing but decorative plants for me. I know there are folks who get all bent out of shape if they lose their roses to mildew, or if their hostas get chewed up by slugs, but I can't muster the same ire over those losses. There are exceptions, of course. I've transplanted peonies from my old house in Virginia, and they make me very happy, and we have lilies from Rachael's childhood house in Richmond. I love my lilac bushes. But if I lose a bunch of daisies to aphids, I can shrug it off.

Two years went by, and I gleefully planted no food. It was a relief. It's nice not to worry about the rain. But I'm back.

I'm back to it for a number of reasons, the first of which is that West needs to garden. Cooking with kids is important, and gardening with them is equally so. It's a cliché to say that we have moved, culturally, into a place where we think that food actually comes from the store. That's not true of West—the boy looks at a deer standing on the side of the road and asks me if we can shoot it so we can eat it. He gets it. He's gathered eggs and he's cooked with me, and we talk constantly about food. But he doesn't like vegetables much—or fruit for that matter. He once gagged and spit up at his preschool while eating *orange slices.* As I planned out the garden—where the new beds would be and what would be in them—I made sure to consult with him. We talked about how we would plant, what we would plant, and I gave him lots of options. I also made sure that one plot—a galvanized tub—was his alone. We planted peas in it for the shoots (his favorite green). You can plant them in a pot, and they'll be up in no time, and they are wonderful when fresh and short to eat in salads or wilted in a pan and drizzled with a touch of sesame oil. Once they sprouted, he was constantly running out to the back deck to grab a few pea shoots and munch them out of hand. As they got taller, West declared he wanted the peas, too. I meant to trellis them, but I just let them fall over the tub and cascade onto the deck, where they seemed pretty happy. He'll munch right through the sugar snaps, I'm sure. We also had a pretty cool outbreak of wild strawberries around the yard, which we transplanted into the other half of the tub.

I didn't do it all on account of a grade-school this-is-where-veggies-come-from project, however. There are deeper reasons to garden. I've learned a lot about our soil recently. At the 2012 TedxManhattan conference titled "Changing the Way We Eat," I learned that it took millions of years to build up our soil and that in the last seventy or so, since the beginning of industrial farming, we've depleted more than half of it.

After World War II, the American government found itself with immense stockpiles of nitrogen, which had been used to make weapons. Nitrogen, after all, is key to making stuff blow up. This surplus is the beginning of the industrial farming age: the feds began suggesting that it be used to grow crops. This dovetailed nicely with the grand American project of deracination that sprouted from the GI Bill. It was certainly a generous program—it's hard to argue on an individual level with the idea that we should send our soldiers to college or give them access to mortgages and so forth after they finish their service. But it decentralized communities and pulled people away from their roots, out into the suburbs where they would work at a growing and increasingly abstract system of paper jobs. We moved folks to Levittown, and we told them that their grandma's cooking had too much garlic in it. New, clean food was to come from the grocery store, and the grocery store would be supplied by industrial farmers, fertilizing their grains with nitrogen, which would be provided cheaply by the feds. The world of tomorrow had arrived, in which the children of immigrants would forget their traditions, their connections, their flavors, and their homegrown skills and replace them with a sharp eye for what was on sale at the new supermarkets that were the cornerstones of the suburban developments across the nation.

In retrospect, it's hard to see why people took the bait. It seems to me that if one set the Jetsons' food pills as an aspirational model, I'd walk right back to Grandma's Sunday gravy and learn how to grow my own greens and make my own sausage. But it must have been a tempting lure: all those shiny appliances and no need to hoe the dirt or work the steam bath in a hot kitchen at the end of the summer.

Miles of tradition were lost. The reason we now fetishize the old ways, line our bookcases with regional cookbooks, and flock to restaurants that offer authenticity is that we chucked it all as the American middle class moved out of city neighborhoods, away from traditions, and into the suburbs.

Of course, some things did need cleaning up. Some of the changes that took away our food heritage needed to happen, and much of what we lost was so criminal, negligent, or diseased that it seems clear that the Jetson-style food pill and the homogenized, pasteurized, uniform products of the suburban grocery store were welcome. Bobrow-Strain wrote in *White Bread* that "in the late nineteenth and early twentieth centuries, city residents got their milk from fetid, overcrowded 'swill dairies' or off unrefrigerated train cars traveling overnight from the surrounding country side. Until mandated pasteurization, milk was a key vector for typhoid and other serious diseases." Even worse are the descriptions of urban bakeries, enhanced by sensationalist reformers but no doubt based upon something true. Bread was churned out of "vermin infested caves with raw sewage dripping from pipes into dough mixing troughs, street dust and horse manure blown onto dough, bread cooling on dirt floors. . . . In the worst cases, bakers worked ankle deep in water and sewage when storms backed up city drains."

This is the sort of stuff one should remember when someone drifts into a romanticized vision of eating like our grandparents did.

The long-term cost of industrializing our food and farming was staggering, and we have only begun to see the ramifications. According to a talk given by Dave Llewellyn, who works at Glynwood Farm just up the road from me, a vegetable today, if bought from the supermarket, has about 40 percent of the nutrients that the same vegetable would have had in the 1930s. To keep the doctor away with apples, you'd have to eat not one, but six. And the methods by which our produce sections are stocked are repellent. To stock the shelves with these faux fruits, these absurd imitations, we've enslaved and poisoned thousands of people and depleted our land.

So I plant. But the garden isn't going to sustain us. I work tiny beds; the kale that I harvest is a hobby: Where am I going to get the rest of it? I did two things.

Dave Llewellyn runs a CSA at Glynwood, and I joined it. I have had, in the past, a pretty strong list of reasons not to join one, and I had to really think it through and find one that I thought would work. I am, by nature, a market shopper—meaning I drift to the store without a preconception of what we should eat for dinner, and I build the meal off of what looks good or what's on sale. There is no "Thursday night is Taco Night" calendar around here. I'm influenced by the season, but I buy precisely what I want. My proclivities could be tuned to the production of a CSA, but it was going to take some effort to relax and let the harvest decide what was on the table. I quickly found that the sense of community, the simple action of driving out to an idyllic farm and smiling at the other members and chatting with the farmer outweighed whatever I'd lost by not having poblano peppers exactly when I wanted them.

I wasn't at all comfortable, either, with the caveat that comes with CSA membership: sharing in the risks of agriculture. If the crops fail, in other words, I don't get what I paid for. The trick is, it seems to me, to find a CSA where the farmers are good at what they do. Dave and Glynwood fulfilled that requirement.

I also rented a plot up the hill on a dirt road where a local woman (named the same as one of the roads that climbs that hill) had cordoned off a bit of land to share. I was told there would be composted manure from her horses and a hose, and I figured I could plant a mess of paste tomato plants there—not the kind you slice for BLTs, which we'd never eat in time, but the kind you can grind and sauce and can and have around for a while. This would free me from one major bit of paranoia. It seems that the canned tomato—a product of which I am not alone in adoration— is one of the worst things you can eat.

First, there's the bisphenol A in the linings of the cans. Dip your toe in the tides of BPA research and you'll find that the undertow of controversy will pull your shoe right off your foot. Studies are done, studies are refuted, claims are made, and products are redesigned. Water bottles hit the shelf proudly displaying that they are BPA-free. This organic compound—meaning carbon based, not Tilth approved—is used in the production of resins, polycar- bonates, and plastics. BPA is very similar, chemically, to estrogen: it basically is a synthetic hormone. Plastics with BPA can break down, leach into food, and according to some studies, disrupt endocrines, especially estrogen. The acidity of tomatoes hurries this breakdown and leaching of BPA into the food. The studies are not conclusive: it might cause changes in brain growth, it might cause breast cancer, it might cause testicular cancer, it may limit sperm growth. It might not. Or maybe we don't eat enough of it to do these things. Is this the level at which we want our decisions about the foods we eat to be made? Is it comforting to hear that while some scientists think it's deadly, other scientists think it isn't?

I would suggest that this is beside the point. I want neither to defend nor condemn the canned tomato, because all I am defending or condemning at that point is a process far removed from my own hands, in which corporations may or may not be using chemicals in the packing of the tomatoes that are detrimental to the health of my family.

What's more, the packing is but the last step in a long

process. One can buy tomatoes in glass, and although it's expensive, it'll be BPA-free. The tomatoes will, however, be grown in such a way that is detrimental to the soil, detrimental to the flavor of the fruit, and detrimental, most of all, to the farm workers who slave—and I mean this word far too literally—in the tomato fields. Barry Estabrook wrote an eye-opening, shocking book, *Tomato-land*, in which he illuminated the practices of the Florida tomato industry. Things there are as bad as they get: poisons so toxic they're outlawed in any other context are routinely sprayed on tomato crops by workers who are not warned of the toxicity, much less protected from it. Workers are exploited in ways that are reminiscent of coal camps. They rent living areas that are dangerous and overcrowded. There exists almost no infrastructure to support the tenants. The systems by which those workers acquire goods and services are internal—that is, you work to pay the debt to the company store, which is, it goes without saying, the *only* store. Estabrook was writing about slicing tomatoes, but how different can it be? I could spend my time finding the best tomatoes to buy, digging around in the literature until I found the organic, fair-trade tomato . . . but why bother? I was thinking of working out some sort of arrangement with a local farm, some setup by which I could buy cases of their bruised and overripe fruit—the kind of fruit no one wants to buy but which makes great sauce—when, deus ex machina, a neighbor told me that there was a plot available up the hill. Why not simply plant them?

Because it was a fool's errand. It was already early July. My six tomato plants at home, in a new raised bed with a subterranean irrigation system I'd rigged by running a fat drainage pipe with the end sticking out in the bottom of it, were all in their first fruit set. The plot up the hill was still covered in weeds, waist-high grass, and tangles of clover. It was worth a shot. And it would be great fun if it worked.

Even as I pulled the weeds with Rachael I began to feel the satisfaction that comes from pushing one's fears away, from doing the right thing. I've become so tied up in this idea—that there is a system of kashrut, that many of the foods we blithely eat are the wrong types of food to be eating—that it has become exactly what I am trying to avoid: a source of great anxiety.

We have been raised in fear: the late sixties—that is, right before my parents had me, the years that formed their mind-set as parents—were terrifying.* The good stuff was over; there were no more flowers. There was just Altamont and speed freaks, gangs, and Manson.

Hunter S. Thompson caught a glimpse of what was coming, I think, when he asked in *Generation of Swine*, "What do you say, for instance, to a generation that has been taught that *rain is poison* and *sex is death?*"

Sex has been deadly since I was old enough to think about it. Rain has been poison since I was a kid. What Richard Hofstadter called the paranoid style in politics became the only operational mode. There's no room for mediation in Hofstadter's analysis of the American political mind-set. It's all or nothing, it's always the End of the World, and the opposing forces, whomever they may be, are bringing it to bear. The way to get elected, Hofstadter illuminated, was to claim that you were standing at the gates, the sole defender of the future. Not only was

*I've come to believe that parenting fixes one, at least a little. Whatever you were thinking about when your baby was born becomes one of your primary modes of thought. It's my way of explaining the generation gap.

he right in his analysis, the paranoid style has become the *only* style. If the only cultural manifestations of this were some songs about death, some fatalistic paintings, and a few deeply troubled New Journalists, that'd be one thing. But the sense has spread that the end is nigh, and our history begins to look—if you're in the wrong mood—like a huge dialectical march toward ruin. We progress from thesis to antithesis to synthesis to a new thesis, from A to B to C to X, but X isn't an improvement; it's a catastrophe.

That vegetables are poison really comes as no surprise. I know, for it's all I've ever been told, that everything I eat will kill me. Eggs, fat, meat, charcoal, nonorganic potatoes, nonorganic apples. And of course, it is within my lifetime that public relations firms really came into their own. They pitched the paranoid style in politics, and they pitched the paranoid style in the supermarket, because if you can make everyone believe that BPA is going to make their children cancerous, stupid, and sterile, they'll flock to the store to buy the new BPA-free water bottles.

The problem is that when they spouted their fearmongering line about how we are eating poison, they weren't wrong. It was a rare marriage of the paranoid style, the fringe, and big-money marketing with the most effective propaganda of all: reality. When you tell me that the waving fields of grain are a poisonous manifestation of corporate greed, that a field of corn is a destructive monocrop that is ruinous to the natural order, I say, *Of course it is.* That's the truth that's been waiting to be revealed. That's the deepest image I have: it's the severed ear on the lawn during the opening of *Blue Velvet*, insisting that all is not right, no matter how it seems on the surface. (And not, mind you, the agitated, unfaithful sigh that is the *wrong* in Cheever stories. We're talking about suburbs where there are body parts strewn about.) It's the fires of Los Angeles revealing to Joan Didion that everyone had always known the city would burn. It's the terrible truth, revealed. The soil is dead, the plants are mutants, and everything we eat will kill us.

It's enough to bring out the Digger in me, to make me not just want to try to do better but to imagine it as a noble feat, a battle. We can grow our own. We can eschew the systems that sell us the poison fruit. We can try. See this? This is my middle finger and this is my hoe, raised up like a battle flag.

Now: Would my tender paste tomatoes make it?

CHAPTER SIX

A Visit with John

W HEN I DROVE TO VIRGINIA and made a handshake deal indicating that the steer with the yellow tag numbered 879 in his ear was mine, I didn't think I'd have much of a relationship with John Whiteside, the owner of Wolf Creek Farm and the man who bred and had raised him thus far. I made some notes and enjoyed my time with John, but I treated it as a passing transaction—a particularly interesting purchase, to be sure, but just that. The idea was that Nathan and I would do the bulk of the work. The steer would be ours. It didn't work out that way.

The first invoice John sent me went whizzing off into cyberspace somewhere, and we had a short season of mutual suspicion in which I wondered why he hadn't billed me and he wondered why I hadn't paid him.

John thought, for a moment, that I didn't want to go through with the purchase. Nathan corrected him. But John showed no interest in moving the steer into Nathan's care.

Nathan called and said that he'd run into Steve Lamb, the farmhand at Wolf Creek, and asked after my steer.

"We took him outta here."

Nathan didn't know what that meant.

John had promised me that he'd e-mail me an invoice after he'd weighed the steer. The invoice never showed.

The first piece of the puzzle clicked into place when the invoice finally showed up: "I am resending this email as I believe you may not have received the original. I have not yet received your check and Nathan inquired as we moved the grass finishing steers to fresh pastures at Wolf Creek Farm this week."

So "outta here" meant simply to greener pastures—fair enough. The original e-mail was included.

We weighed your steer (ear tag Yellow-879) today and he tipped the scales at 675 pounds. I accessed the sales results for our local livestock salebarn and have attached the results from their most recent sale, held on 30 August 2011. Cattle are sold and priced according to hundred weight (cwt.). Thus, your steer was in the 600-700 range, where 41 animals sold at an average of 663 pounds and $1.275/lb ($127.7/cwt.). I have also attached a copy of your invoice, which reflects the 675 pounds @ $1.275/lb, or a total of $861.97. Please make your check payable to Wolf Creek Farm Production, LC and mail to the address below.

Nathan was not yet prepared to receive your steer (he needs to fix some of his fencing first), so we agreed to put him and his two herd peers with our grass finishing steers which are grazing just across the Rapidan River from Nathan's place. Nathan was able to join us as we were unloading the steers into the pasture and he took a few photos. It was drizzling at the time, so I'm not sure how well the pictures will turn out, but no complaints as we certainly need the rain.

During the lag, John had simply assumed I'd changed my mind. In late October, I wrote out the check, typed a letter thanking John for his help, and tucked both into a copy of my last book. I figured Nathan would fix the fences, John would get the check, and all would settle in the way I'd intended.

Only a couple of days passed before I got an e-mail from John.

Max,

I received your package today. Thank you for the check. Your steer is doing well, grazing at Wolf Creek Farm with his peers. I'll try to send you a pic. Thank you also for the copy of "Chasing the White Dog." While you are correct in your observation that the farmer's life leaves little time for the pleasure of reading, I always keep a few books on the bedside table in order that I can sneak in a few pages until my body fails to cooperate. I think I will put your book in my truck so that I can enjoy it during the lull between the 6am setup at the farmer's market and the 7am official opening for customers.

We weaned our spring calves last week. The noise was non-stop for a couple of days, but the cows soon quieted down and focused on gaining condition for the coming winter and next spring's births. The calves took a few more days to settle but now have reestablished themselves as a herd without mamas and have become the mischievous adolescents they will be for the next six months.

We worked one of our two fall herds this week. The dams received their pre-breed vaccines and the calves received their 3-month vaccines and the steer calves were banded (humane castration, if indeed there is such a thing). The cow-calf pairs were then separated into breeding herds based upon which bull we have selected to breed each cow for calving next fall. Our bulls were given breeding performance tests to ensure their semen has the motility and normality required to assure successful breeding of all dams who come into estrus. We plan to work the other fall herd next week. We will then turn the bulls in with one herd on 1 November and with the other herd on 1 December, and will pull the bulls on 1 January and 1 February respectively. This gives the cows two estrus cycles to conceive (we cull cows who don't conceive) and produces calves in a tight 60-day calving window to facilitate herd management. The 30-day offset on the two fall herds spreads out the calving intensive periods to enable us to spend more time with the herd that requires it, and it also provides us with an additional 30 days of age differential in our ultimate finishing steers to provide more flexibility in beef supply.

We completed the last cutting of hay two weeks ago (our third cutting) and are almost finished moving the hay to position it nearby the pastures through which we plan to rotate the herds this winter and where we want to add more organic matter to the soils by unrolling hay. Next week, we plan to no-till drill annual rye grass seed into one of our "finishing" pastures, which will provide early spring grazing for our finishing steers. The steers are currently grazing their final rotation of the year over our cool season mixed grass pastures. Once they are finished grazing, we plan to fertilize these pastures with crushed rock amendments to provide the correct quantity and balance of the minerals required to produce nutrient dense grasses and beef from the animals who graze these grasses. These pastures will then rest over winter and we will apply manures, aerate, and no-till drill additional cool season perennial seeds early next spring so these pastures are ready for first grazing late spring and early summer. During the winter, the steers will graze stockpiled fescue pastures and receive high nutrient balage which was made from the second hay cutting this past spring.

So, things are starting to wind down on the farm. Just in time for the winter months of fence mending, firewood splitting, hunting, and developing plans for next year. An exhausting occupation, but one which has a peaceful rhythm and a sustainable purpose.

Regards,
John

John Whiteside
Grass Farmer
Thank you for your patronage of Wolf Creek Farm, your local and sustainable source for grassfed natural beef.

I reported the exchange to Rachael happily: *Got a great note from John the Farmer.* (I tag people like that when I'm relaying research information to Rachael; it's always "Whiskey Jake" or "Tomato Joe.") *He told me all about the farm. Boy, it's something getting letters from a Yalie farmer, you know? The thing was probably eight hundred words! Gave me some real insight. Like a farm report.*

"Did he say when he was giving Bubbles to Nathan?"

I looked at the e-mail again—had I missed that piece of information?

Well, no. I mean, he's in touch, you know? He acknowledged payment, after all.

"What are you going to do?"

It's not like he's going to steal him.

This was met with only a chilly stare, like if she simply looked at me long enough, I'd see myself through her eyes and see just how absurd I was being.

I'd paid almost $900 for the right to call Yellow Tag 879 my own, and I couldn't really. I had no idea where he was. I had no idea why he hadn't been delivered. I was flummoxed.

The story of my steer adrift was pretty good fodder for dinner parties. I could relate, over the wine glasses, that I'd spent a ton of money on a third of a ton of beef on the hoof, and I'd subsequently lost it. It drove Rachael insane, of course. I'd chuckle about it—*I have no idea where he is. I mean, I assume he's on the farm somewhere*—and I could see her giving me the eyeballs. You'd have thought I'd come home from poker night with a funny story about losing a thousand dollars. I'd assure her that we'd get him in the end, that the steer would be, in one way or another, returned to his rightful owner, but she couldn't handle the idea that I couldn't say exactly where he was right then.

I had imagined raising a steer with my friend, and lots of drives to Virginia and muddy boots and maybe an emergency that needed attending. I figured I'd get down there for some milestone moments, and Nathan and I would spend some quality time in the field. It wasn't working out that way, but I hadn't given up hope. Surely John would rather move the steer to Nathan's pasture than simply keep him in the herd. Why would he want to work a steer he didn't own? The winter feed wouldn't cost much, and a single animal doesn't really move the bottom line, but you'd think that on principle he wouldn't want to winter the steer over, feed him on his hay, and assume the risk of something terrible happening to Yellow Tag 879. I figured it was just a matter of time, but time came and went.

Over the Christmas holidays, I spent some time with Nathan and his family on the farm. We walked the woods a bit, sighted in my rifle, and looked for but didn't see any deer. I had hoped to visit John, and I wrote him. We left the specific time up in the air and failed to get together. I noticed, however, that when I'd asked about visiting, there hadn't been any mention of moving the animal, any suggestion that Nathan had anything to do with the project at all.

Spring bloomed, and I was back in Virginia visiting family. I asked John out to lunch.

John Whiteside is tall and pale, with a windblown, outdoorsy complexion and a penchant for khakis and floppy-brimmed hats. There's a slight hitch in his walk, and his shoulders are broad. When younger, he was a horseman and rowed crew, and one can see in his movements a residual athletic ropiness, no doubt maintained by years of farm work. He wears button-down shirts, and he drives a Ford four-wheel-drive pickup truck that's old enough for him to have to get out and unlock the hubs when he drives on asphalt. He's thin of lip and high of cheekbone—hinting at the high WASP in his past. He squints when he talks.

The only evidence, other than the hundreds of acres he calls his own, of his past business with the robber baron classes (a stint at Bain Capital, a Harvard MBA, mergers and acquisitions at MCI before the scandalous meltdown) is the utter confidence with which he speaks. He does not dither or wait to see if you're going to agree. He talks like a man who has had the last word for quite some time.

"There are three types of people coming into farming, now," he said over a spinach salad at the Madison Inn. The first group, he explained, are the young inheritors, people who have taken up the family farm. They are going to sell into the market, not create a new one. If beef prices are high (which they were when we met, as a result of a drought in the southern plains and increased overseas demand for American beef), these farmers will jump into the market and sell. They aren't necessarily looking at farming practices, trying to create sustainable systems, or shepherding the land.

"Then you've got the young adventurers," said John. Maybe they inherited some money, maybe they made some, and they want to start a farm. "They are sprinters; they cycle through in three or four years." He gets calls from young start-up farmers all the time, and he isn't impressed. They don't understand the pace of farming, he said. They don't understand how slow you have to move and how much there is to figure out. They are sophomoric, he suggested without calling them that exactly, and they ring him up and announce all their sweeping plans and grand ideas, none of which have anything to do with how they are going to manage their herd, how they are going to get their water, or what their breeding program is going to be. Then they get up at 4:00 a.m. for a few years, and they tire of it.

The third group are the second-career guys, the John Whitesides of the world, who start with capital from another venture; some of them are succeeding. They have to know what they are getting into. They have to think like endurance athletes—constant training, constant readiness, and in it for the long haul. Otherwise, John said, they'll "come in, blow a fortune, and get out."

It took John eight years to find a farm. He'd been working in Herndon and living deeper into Virginia, and he liked it. He wanted a farm that was close to a college town, where there would be an educated market receptive to local, responsibly grown food.

"Local starts in college towns," he said.

He had other requirements, as well:

"Water had to rise on the farm. It couldn't have any run-off from the surrounding land," because you can't control what the people around you are putting on their land or in their water. Water rights aren't typically much of an issue on the East Coast, but John has a streak of survivalist mentality in him, and I'm sure that he would find a water supply that was downstream of someone else, a fount in someone else's control, unbearable.

"It needed to have clean soil, which meant no crops, no orchards. It couldn't have been planted. And it needed good woodlands, which retain water in the winter."

Crops and orchards are heavy users of pesticides, and John didn't want to inherit someone's tainted land. Land without woods will simply dry up because there aren't trees to store the water. But if you start with broad strokes like that, you realize you've quickly removed a lot of land from the market; you've narrowed your potential purchases down to a sliver of what's available.

He found Wolf Creek Farm, about 330 acres in thirty parcels, which had been operating as a seed-stock farm for Limousin bulls. A seed-stock enterprise is on the fancy end of the cattle business, and the farm was a little bit of a showplace, with graceful white fences. He didn't need the fancy bits, but everything else was just right. Finding the farm was just the beginning.

"It takes thirty months to get a calf on the ground, and it's one hundred months before you can see whether you're headed in the right direction [with a herd]. It takes seven or eight years to get the land right, and it's probably ten years before you really know if you're headed in the right direction."

Why do it?

"It's the right thing to do," said John without hesitation. "I do it for the community, for the psyche, and for the stomach—for mine and for theirs. And for the cattle."

Out in the fields, John is at home. He is happy to see his cattle, and he clucks and calls at them. As we drove the pastures, he slowed to check up on little things—a glance here, a glance there; he looked at a fence, a heifer, a well. He took me to the herd of steers nearing their market weight, and they happily approached the truck. Yellow Tag 879 was right there, standing in the middle, gazing at us, bright eyed. He was bigger than when I'd seen him last. He weighed 905 pounds when last on the scale. He'd gained an average of 1.44 pounds per day. His forehead was broad, and the fur there was matted and twisted in a cowl. This was evidence of the way he felt about himself, if such a thing can be said.

"He's been feeling himself," said John, meaning that the steer was coming into his own, feeling confident and big and mildly aggressive. "He's bigger than a lot of these steers, and he's acting like a bull. They butt things."

As a group, the steers looked healthy and happy. They clomped over the tall, thick grass and surrounded the truck, pooling all around us—it reminded me of the stories my dad would tell of Vali, the famous witch of Positano, Italy, who was a friend of his and for a while a cause célèbre (George Plimpton produced a movie about her. Mick Jagger loved her. There's a great book of photos called *Love on the Left Bank* about her time in Paris as a hash-smoking young actress). She would walk to a stream in the cliffs where she lived and wiggle her fingers in the water. Trout would swim up and swirl around her, much like men swam up and swirled around her weird little compound. The steers pooled around the truck; they were almost menacing in their groupthink, their seeming determination, and their sheer mass. They smelled grassy, fresh, and clean, and they were, in as much as one can say this, happy to see us. Their breath smelled like fermenting grass; their shit smelled like pasture.

When John had called out to some steer, months before when he was showing me around, they'd all walked right up to the fence. There's a delicate bit of training involved in getting a herd to respond that way. They are prey animals, and if they are frightened of you, they will avoid you. It doesn't take much to turn them against you, and they will not forget it. A predator—dogs, for instance—will forgive you. (That's why bird dogs have collars that deliver quick electric shocks. They will yelp, and then they will come sulking back to you, wanting to win you back. If you were to try the same tactic on a cow, the cow would never get near you again.) I recalled another moment in a Virginia pasture, when I was following a fox hunt. I was in a truck with one of the whips (the riders who help the huntsman and work for the hunt, often well out in front, are called "whippers-in," often shortened to "whips"), and he'd done something that might spook some cattle. The landowner was nearby, and he dressed that man down, exclaiming that they'd been trained to come to people, come to the truck, and if they were frightened now, a year of work would be undone. There are no second chances, and being able to approach cattle is a key aspect of being able to farm them.

Out there, in the tall grass, the cattle surrounded John, and he waxed on about his bigger motivations: "I'm using cattle to steward the land. One thing we can do is what we do to the land."

He enjoys it. "No two years are the same—no two *days* are the same." He turned again to athletic metaphor: "Farming is like a sport; you've got to harvest the energy of the game." Lots of farmers, he explained, stick to the regimen. They've got a plan—a grazing plan, for instance, of where the cattle will graze and when mapped out on a computer—and they stick to it. John doesn't think you can do that. You've got to feel the energy of the farm and use what you know to make fluid, informed decisions. John thinks that we've made horrible choices, historically, and that we may not recover from them. Big corporations are insulated from the effect their products have on the world, and capital is allowed to work silently for itself. I saw, as the conversation went on, that there is a secular millenarian underpinning to much of what John says. Huge transformations—not good ones—seem very possible to him.

"Part of what I'm doing, part of why I'm here, is that when it all hits the fan, I want this place to be a seed. Something mankind can pick up and start from."

He's hopeful, too: "People are realizing that you really can control your life, but you have to be an active participant."

We drove back up to the main house, a low white building with lots of flowers planted around it.

"So, what do you want to do with him? He'll be ready in three months."

I was caught off guard—this was months ahead of our original schedule. I asked if we were going to move him over to Graves Mill, and John said he didn't think it was a good idea. The steer was happy, he was with a herd, and the owners of Graves Mill wouldn't be too enthusiastic about hosting a steer there, anyway.

So that was it—landowner politics. I had heard, in fact, that John had tried to rent pasture from Graves Mill but that the deal, for one reason or another, hadn't flown. John said something about how he'd rather not, really, kick that hornet's nest.

I asked him if that was okay, him working a steer he didn't own. I didn't want to put him out.

"It's a onetime thing. It'll be fine. Just figure out what you want to do with him. You've got ninety days."

When we first met, 879's schedule had put him at harvest weight in October; now his deadline was July. I was not ready.

CHAPTER SEVEN

To Catch What Cannot Be Seen

IT'S A DIFFICULT THING TO SAY that one loves to fish— who would dare? I hear immediately a chorus of naysayers—"Do you, now?"—and they are right in doubting. For love is often understood as something on a spectrum, and the proof of it is in the devotion and sacrifice, the obsessive dedication. How can I even think such a thing— that I *love* fishing—in a world that has seen the likes of John D. Voelker, author of *Trout Madness* and *Anatomy of a Murder*? That man loved to fish. Hemingway loved to fish. That guy at the dock, with the deep tan and the leathery skin, drinking a tall-boy Coors Light at 11:00 a.m. and wearing neoprene boots—he loves to fish more than I do, and he is better at it, and he has spent geometrically more time with a fishing rod in his hand than I have. So I don't mean to say that I love fishing in the way that these folks do, or anywhere approaching it, and I don't mean to say that I am good at fishing, or that I even do much of it. I've spent too much time in libraries, too much time in cocktail bars, too much time playing guitar, and too much time with my son at the playground to qualify for the club. But I love it. I love the way a tackle box smells of old plastic heated by the sun, dried-out soft bait, and salmon eggs. I love looking at the water and wondering what's down there. I love dreaming of monsters lurking in the depths, and I love occasionally pulling one of their smaller cousins up into the air. I like the flow and arc of a well-thrown cast. I love how one is moved from a meditative state— all rhythmic reeling in and casting and staring into the totally foreign, unavailable world—into blood-surging, adrenaline-fueled thrill the second the strike pulls down the tip of the rod. (It is said that this rush fades over time, just as it is supposed to in hunting, replaced, I guess, by calm and systematic expertise. I hope that's not the case.) I love fishing, and I want to do more of it.

I also love eating fish, and while everyone knows that fish is better fresh, most people don't understand how fresh it can be. Steven Rinella, in his book *Meat Eater*, wrote, "Too bad that the taste of fresh fish doesn't last. In fact, you can watch the quality of a freshly caught salmon deteriorate right before your eyes. Flop one into your canoe on a hot, sunny day and it begins to spoil within minutes. . . . Suddenly you realize that the black bears you were watching had it figured out: eat the fish as soon as it's caught, all the better if it's still in the water."

If you want real fish, then you have to pull it out of the water yourself.

I also think—I might even know it—that fishing is good for kids. It's a great way to become accustomed to sharp tools and to learn that you might try and try at something, you might do everything you are supposed to do, and it may not work out. And it is far, far slower than anything else kids get up to.

That said, lots of kids don't quite cotton to it. West seems to enjoy fishing in theory, but not in actuality. By the time I was his age—six years old as I type—I had already spent more time fishing than anything except going to school or sleeping. West wants to go fishing, but so far he doesn't really want to fish. I'm just going to keep taking him and see if a switch flips.

One cold and windy day in early May, West and I met some friends on the Cold Spring waterfront to throw some lures for striper. The striped bass spends most of its life in salt water, but it swims up into the fresh waters of the Hudson (as well as the Delaware River and the Chesapeake and Massachusetts Bays) to spawn. They hit the Hudson in the spring, following the herring upstream, and can be very big: the record for a fish caught on tackle is 81.8 pounds. They are fast and sleek, with bright silvery-white bellies that glow with a hint of golden yellow. The scales are mostly silver, and they get their name from the seven or eight charcoal stripes that run from the gills to the tail on both sides. To my eye, they are perfectly proportioned: the angle from the pelvic fins and the dorsal fin to the mouth is even and smooth, and the mouth itself is central, what's known as "terminal" (as opposed to the upturned mouth, called superior, or the subterminal, inferior, mouth of bottom-feeders). They seem to frown ever so slightly because of their strong maxilla. The tail is homocercal, made of balanced triangles. They are hungry fish, not as indiscriminate as a bluefish, but predatory as hell. Big stripers will fight hard enough to have you messing with the drag on the reel and giving them some room to move before they tire out. They tend to dive, which gives the fight a weighty, steady feel.

There was a storm passing by that day, and although it was very far away, out in the ocean, the tail of it was dragging across us, and the winds were hard and steady coming down the river. They were so strong that we had to shout to hear one another, and really, you'd have thought that we *knew* something about the habits of striper in great wind.

Oh, sure, once you see the wind sock ripped off the flagpole, you've got to get down there. In a wind like that, striper will bite on anything. Throw a shoe in there and Bob's your uncle.

Of course, this isn't true. We were just unlucky when we threw a dart at the calendar and said we'd all go fishing on Sunday.

The kids all had little spinning rods, and the grown-ups had slightly bigger rigs, and we were casting and laughing and hollering to one another over the gusts. Occasionally, someone would run off and sit in his vehicle just to warm up and get a break from the pressure of the bluster that was surging down the river. I'd brought some sandwiches, and the kids all ate them while sitting in our town's little waterfront gazebo. Nobody was catching anything, and after they ate, the kids didn't want anything more to do with the rods, so they climbed on the town cannon (we made the Parrot gun here, a small-bore rifled cannon, which is thought to have been the deciding factor in the Union victory at Gettysburg) and chased each other and laughed and shrieked.

Just as I was thinking that the wind wasn't worth it, that this was tiring, and that the kids were probably getting cold, my tip bent and the line pulled and I moved to set the hook. Ain't it always the way? As soon as you move to pack it in, something happens. Bang—I was hooked up. The surge of adrenaline subsided somewhat when I realized that I was not hooked up on a striper. Reeling this fish in felt like reeling in a heavy boot. It seemed like it might want to swim away, but it wasn't sure of it.

Of course even the dullest fish is hard to move through the water, and I was reeling it in for a few minutes.

Just before I got it to the surface, I heard behind me the sound to which all parents are most keenly attuned: my child in pain.

I snapped around to see what had happened and registered that West had fallen and, from the looks of it, had fallen hard. I could see his shoe a few feet behind him and realized that he'd been running and lost it or tripped over it, and now he was shaking and crying and holding himself on the cold bricks.

It was hard to be heard over the wind, which added a certain operatic melodrama to the proceeding, but I managed to get one of the kid's attention: *There's a fish on here. Reel him in!*

He looked confused for a moment, but I know he likes to fish, and he got to it. Walking over to West across the little plaza that is our waterfront, I told the father of the boy now holding my rod to go help him, that there was a fish on that line. His confusion lingered longer than his kid's had, and he looked as if he wanted to talk about the process, maybe get a list of possible outcomes, or set up a good strategy. I didn't stop walking—my son was in pain on the ground, after all. I just shot him a look that I hoped conveyed a need for him to simply rise to the moment. West was fine, although he'd fallen from a headlong run and from the looks of the round indentation with little dots of blood on his knee, he'd fallen on a bottle cap. I hugged him and told him he was okay and did that weird thing we do where we rub up and down on a person's arms, sort of warming them up. I sat with him a while with my arm around him, reassuring him and promising that we could go home. After he was calm, I told him I'd had a fish on the line when he fell and suggested we check it out. I got his shoe and put it on him, helped him up, and we walked over hand in hand to check out the catch.

The father-and-son team I'd left in charge had landed the fish and plopped it in a puddle right there on the bricks, where it panted. It was a bullhead catfish, all slimy brown and round bodied like a fat cigar, with its crazy Dalí mustache shooting out of either side of its mouth. It was about a foot long, and I think they'd meant the puddle as a bit of mercy: "Oh, there's some water—let's put it there until Max gets over here to tell us what to do." It looked odd, this fish in a puddle, and I couldn't help but shake my head. They could have simply thrown it right back in. They sure as hell didn't need me to tell them that I wasn't going to keep a Hudson River bullhead. I guess it's honorable, though, not throwing back another man's fish.

Of all the fish you could drag out of the Hudson, the bullhead is perhaps the least appealing. Maybe it's even with the eel. Russell caught an eel in a crab trap once, right at the same spot on the waterfront where I got the bullhead, and watching it swerve and dance in the trap was downright creepy. Of course, I would overcome creepy if it wasn't common knowledge that eels and catfish, bottom dwellers in a profoundly polluted river, are not to be eaten. The levels of toxicity are too high. Those fish are poison.

Although we threw back the bullhead, it felt good to catch something. Unfortunately, that was all I reeled out of the Hudson during the striper season of 2012. It occurred to me that I should learn more about what stripers do—I know they like bloodworms and herring, and I know they like to feed on things washed down to them as the tide rolls out. They are lazy, and they like to sit in deep water in front of an obstruction. But knowing all that had caught me a bullhead. Maybe I'd be better prepared when they came back down the river in the fall.

OVER THE PAST FEW YEARS, Rachael, West, and I, with a few families from our town, have established a tradition of spending a week in the summer on Block Island. It's a peaceful, unpretentious place off the shore of Rhode Island, and we can drive there in half a day. We have a lot of dinner parties while we're there, and the kids all play together in the sand. We drink too much and get sunburns. We go in late August, summer's last hurrah.

While we're there, Russell and Sharr White and Dick Gordon and I spend one morning out on Captain Chris Willi's boat fishing. We arrive at the dock about half an hour before dawn (dark thirty, generally speaking, is when the hunt for anything should begin) and hop on Willi's twenty-six-foot Regulator with two 225-horsepower Yamahas hanging off the back. Our first time out, after one look at those engines, I knew exactly what we were in for. I threw Russell a grin, wondering if Sharr and Dick had ever gone as fast in a boat as we were about to go. (You've got four hours, the thinking goes, and you don't want to spend the bulk of that time getting to your spot.) We burbled our way to the Block Island Sound, pointing at a lighted buoy so distant I was impressed the captain could see it at all. It was falsely comforting, rocking gently through the no-wake zone, protected by the natural harbor, watching the sun crack through the edge of the horizon. When we hit the open water, the captain shoved the throttles forward and we took off over what was suddenly pretty rough sea. The little boat leapt over the troughs— four feet? Six feet?—and slammed into the swells, torquing and jumping off of the next peak, spraying us with salt water as our kidneys were pounded and our hands gripped whatever they could. It was the sort of ride where one begins the internal monologue about how the boat was manufactured to handle this. Boats just don't snap in half . . . do they? This guy does this all the time, right? Twice a day? He knows what he's up to. It's not like the boat is going to simply shatter. Right? Right?

Our first time out, I caught nothing. I learned the following year that Willi had told my story all year long. I was the guy who couldn't hook one. I was losing lures, and the fish were hitting me but not getting on my hooks. Willi, sympathetic, tried to attract some fish by throwing a hookless lure like a white torpedo that rushed along the surface. His cast was tremendous. He can cast farther than I can accurately shoot. He whipped the lure along, and the idea was that the fish would chase it, see my lure, and bite. The fish followed, but they didn't go for me. I had an irreversible stink on me that day. But I caught a glimpse of something I'll never forget. Willi brought in his lure with two mammoth fish chasing it, and I watched them, near the surface, flashing their white bellies, swimming like fighter jets in formation. They came up close to the surface, right at my feet, and seemed to break to either side like the Blue Angels peeling off one another, and just as fast. It made one think about what lives in the water. When I was a kid, my family went fishing off the coast of Florida on a party boat. While we were out there, a giant manta ray—twenty feet across?—slammed into the side of our boat, pushing it hard to the side and then slipping away through the water like a UFO.

There are some heavy beasts hidden down there.

Dick caught a monster of a striper that first year—upwards of fifty pounds, the sort of catch that gets put up on the charter website to advertise that they know where to hook 'em—and Russell and Sharr both caught smaller ones. A few bluefish were brought on deck as well.

We ate them all. I stopped the captain before he chucked the whole frame of Dick's big striper to the gulls and had him cut out the cheeks. They were the size of the soft part of my palm, and Russell and I ate them off the cutting board back at our house with wasabi and some soy sauce I'd packed in a flash of foresight. (*Pace* Dick, I don't know how the cheeks ended up in our bag of fish.) We grilled the bluefish over coals that very night. (Their flavor deteriorates quickly, though our captain was smart and knew to bleed them out in the ocean water as soon as they were caught so they would taste a little fresher, more gentle.) If eaten soon, they aren't too oily, but rather have enough fat and juice to stand up to the hot smoke off the grill. The striper became seviche, diced to the size of the first joint of my thumb and marinated in limes and lemons until it was "cooked," then mixed with green tomatoes, a sweet red pepper, and a Vidalia onion all cut in a fine dice. We invited everyone we knew who was on the island, filled up a big table with friendly faces, and spooned out helpings of amazingly fresh fish over crusty bread while we drank pitchers of rum punch.

We were back the following year, in calmer water, and my lines were tight. I pulled a thirty-four-inch blue, the first on the boat.

The blue is a sleeker fish than the striper. Shaped like a hungry sports car, it has dorsal and anal fins that almost mirror one another and are placed back toward the oversize, pointy tail. They look fast and mean, which they are, and they shimmer like smooth, blue stainless steel.

Once my fish was on the boat, Russell called out a congratulatory rib about having broken last year's curse, and Willi looked over at me and said, "Oh! That was you! I've been telling that story all year, about this one guy I took out who could not catch a single fish."

Russell, Willi, and I were all relieved that fish were not permanently adverse to my hooks—Willi, because it must suck to bring people out and take their money and not get them hooked up; me, for obvious reasons; and Russell, because it was his idea to go fishing in the first place, and he can't stand it if things don't work out. Most fishermen are fiercely competitive, and it takes a serious measure of self-control to suppress the impulse. Russell is competitive, but he's also self-aware and generally well wishing enough to stop the impulse. Many are not. Hemingway, for instance, once shot the sharks that were going after a marlin that his fishing buddy had caught (and which looked bigger than anything Hem had caught himself). He shot them off the back of the *Pilar* with a tommy gun, under the pretense of protecting the catch. What happened, and Hem must have known this would happen, is that the shot sharks bled into the water and attracted *more* sharks, and they ate most of the big fish right off the line. When they got to the dock, the marlin couldn't be weighed or measured. That's unacceptably competitive, if not psychopathically competitive. Most fishermen manage to begrudgingly congratulate those by whom they are bested and then simply smolder in the knowledge that they themselves are the better angler. They'll attempt to prove it at the next opportunity or, in the tradition of fishermen everywhere, simply lie to make up the difference in the quantity or size of the catch.

We hooked a few and moved on to the next spot. I enjoy the breaks in between casting: the boat wide open, splashing through the swells, and all of us finally awake enough to start talking.

"What makes a fish a bait fish?" Dick asked me.

I answered that it was simply anything smaller than what you were fishing for. If you're fishing for sharks, then the fish we were catching were bait fish. Look at the food chain and move down the ladder one step: that's bait fish.

The second year we were out, Willi had thrown a white beanbag on deck (nautical beanbags—who knew?), and it was fun to sit on and even more fun to envision it bouncing off of the bow of the boat and watching someone get taken by the wind like a cartoon—*whoosh!*—to bob on a beanbag in the water behind us while we circled back around.

Willi eased the throttles, the boat slid down off its plane, the prow level once again, and we all stood up and reached for our rods. There was a *phffft phfffft phffft phfffft* sound off the port side, where silvery menhaden a little longer than your hand were leaping into the air. Dozens of them popped out of the water. They only do this when they are being chased, ambushed by game fish that were waiting for them to swim over. Bait don't jump for fun; they jump because something is trying to eat them. Menhaden jump at about a fifteen-degree angle, and they make a good distance. It's hard to judge, but it looks like they get three or four feet of air before slipping back into the water with a tight splash and a wiggle that shoots them forward. There is nothing you can see, with a fishing rod in your hand, that equals a flash like that. It's like seeing the face of your lord in a piece of toast: proof of the unknown, there, tangible, before your eyes. We were momentarily stupefied.

"Get your lines in the water!" called out Willi. "I can't get you any closer than that!"

I cast right into it and hooked up immediately.

We pulled the lips off of fish pretty well all morning. I caught another four after my first big one. Three of us caught thirty-four-inch blues, which are about as big as they get. A thirty-four-inch bluefish would be thirteen or fourteen years old. We felt good about that, but it left us in a quandary, since we'd all thrown money into a pool to be taken by whomever caught the biggest fish. Three of us were tied.

We discussed it on the dock, drinking well-earned 9:30 a.m. Narragansett lagers ("Made on Honor, Sold on Merit"), and it was decided that Sharr, who had missed the tie by an inch or so, would buy us all breakfast.

We ate our fish two nights in a row. The most successful meal was a filet that I rubbed with Old Bay and put in the Camerons smoker—a brilliant contraption: basically a hotel chafing pan with a tight lid that allows you to smoke things on a stovetop—with some alder wood chips. It was tender and fresh, and the spice and the smoke cut right through the fatty flesh.

OUR FOUR FAMILIES spent hours that summer at Town Beach on the ocean side of the island. We had an onshore wind, which kept the waves down to something the kids could play in. Russell and I both brought fishing rods, and whenever there was a break in the beach traffic, we'd cast into the surf. You don't want to hook a kid on a boogie board or get your line tangled in one of the old men who swim steadily just beyond the breakers, crawling parallel to the shore.

I was casting out a big silver lure—metal, spoon shaped, the size of a sardine—and standing just calf deep in the water when I saw a flash out by the buoy.

Thirty, forty, a hundred bait fish, hitting the surface and leaping.

Holy shit. Russell, did you see that?

Again a series of silver reflections broke the surface, and the water frothed to white. This was a feed.

Using information we'd gathered talking to the locals at one of the tackle shops, we figured it must be a school of albacore.

I threw as long and as hard as I could. I'd never make it out to the buoy, but if I could get anywhere near it, well, that kind of distance is nothing for a fast fish. We'd seen bait fish swimming around our knees all day, and someone had seen a striper rolling along behind them in water no deeper than your waist. It was worth a shot. I was walking out into the ocean, not even thinking about it. The waves were crashing into me. I was up to my belly, and the waves were over my head. I held tight to the rod, turned sideways to let the water crash over me, and then cast again toward the fish. The bite was on. The bait were jumping. It was incredible to see—hundreds of fish leaping out of the roiling water in surges.

Water is weird. One of my favorite facts is that if you are parachuting into the ocean, it is almost impossible to tell how far from the surface you are. I think it's generally pretty hard to tell how far away things are unless you're very experienced. The buoy looked to me as if I might be able to get a cast somewhere near it. I figured it was maybe two hundred yards offshore. Later, I wrote Chris Willi and asked him how far out it was. He told me it was three-quarters of a mile.

I heard Russell saying something to my right, and I looked over to see him rowing out astride his stand-up paddleboard. He wasn't standing, but rather riding it like a wide kayak. He couldn't stand because he was bracing his fishing rod to the deck. He paddled right into the thick of it, and I watched him while I casted again. His tip bent. He was hooked up! It lasted only a moment, and then the rod snapped back up.

Back on shore, he was fishless but thrilled: "Did you see that?" He was breathless, pumped up. "I hooked one! The drag was set wrong and he got some slack and he tossed the hook, but I got one on the line out there!"

But . . . then what? What was step two?

A paddleboard is light, after all, and he'd have needed at least one hand to hold on to the rod, both if he tried to reel it in. He would have been dragged out to sea. Or, okay, what if he'd landed it? He'd have a big flapping fish on a surfboard, no tools, no knife: *What? You were going to club it with the paddle?*

"That's not a bad idea, actually."

But it would have been, of course, although it would have been fun to watch.

BACK HOME, I eyed the fly rod that had been leaning in the corner since I talked my dad into giving it to me. He'd gone through a fly-fishing phase, but it seemed to have passed, and I had told him I'd like to learn. There was always something else to do, and it took me a long time, a couple of years, to put it together and start practicing my cast.

Fly-fishing looks like the most complicated business

imaginable, as if those who can do it are in command of some sort of grand physics. I won't say they aren't, but I will say that I got into the timing of the thing fairly easily. I stood in the yard on hot afternoons, and I practiced. I roll casted (which is when you can't flip the line out behind you to shoot it, because, for instance, there are trees behind you). I false casted (which is when you shoot line but you don't let the fly land, because you are going to shoot more line and cast farther). I whipped the whole thing back and forth, just feeling the line in my fingers and trying to get a sense of how to unspool the thick line off of the reel and let it dangle at my feet. I tested myself: Could I put the leader under that bush? (You tie leaders of different sorts to the end of your line, depending on what you're fishing for, looking sometimes for strength, sometimes for stealth. In fly-fishing, you tie a length of leader after the line itself and then tie a tippet after that, each more invisible than the last.) Could I land the leader in that shadow? Underneath the leaves of the apricot tree? Soon I could, and I'd watch the line float out in front of me and land, sometimes in too many coils but sometimes in a way that seemed just right. I casted from different angles in the yard. A neighbor called out to ask if I'd caught anything. (Like my friends, telling one another of the plots I've attempted to include them in, I assume that my neighbors get small kicks out of watching me go about my projects—building chicken coops and patios, casting fly rods, smoking meat by the fifty weight. It's not the best show you could ask for, but it's not too shabby.)

One afternoon, I was feeling good about what I was doing: the line was flowing smoothly, and the tippet was landing where I wanted it to in the yard. There was a weird pull in the middle of the back cast, but I ignored it until the line snagged. There wasn't anything on the end of the leader, so I didn't understand how it could snag at all, and I turned around to look, petulantly, at what was slowing me down, only to discover that I'd wrapped the leader around a power line. The color washed from my face, and I recalled the words my doctor had spoken when I'd called her to ask about the possible effects of a nasty shock I'd received from a wet lamp.

"Well," she said, chuckling, "you're calling me. And that means you're alive. So I'd say you're going to be fine."

I pulled the leader down with a snap and repositioned myself, making a note to look more carefully at where the line went when it arced gracefully over my head, ready for the shoot.

I sent an e-mail to Rory Donovan, who has become, since I wrote about him in *Chasing the White Dog*, a very good friend. He is a serious fisherman. He worked for years as a guide in Colorado and has sold a fly to Orvis. (I have no idea where this falls in the scheme of things. It could be like selling a song to Nashville, or it could be like giving a nickname to a fraternity brother—a source of pride, either way.) He was excited when I told him that I was going to take up the sport and wanted to be kept abreast of the progress. I wrote and said that I'd been practicing my cast in the yard and that I loved it. His reply echoed what Russell had said when I told him I had enjoyed shooting skeet:

"Are you for real? About casting in the yard for two hours being fun? Because if you enjoyed that you may not be able to handle actually casting at fish. It could kill you."

Despite my protestation that I liked process, I was itching to get out on the water. I listened to rumors of forgotten streams and drove slowly by likely locations, looking for any bit of public access but finding mostly yellow posted signs. Were cemeteries posted? Weren't they public by definition? (No, they aren't.) What if I was standing in the creek itself? Isn't water always public? (Nope.)

Late at night, I pored over the Department of Environmental Conservation maps, looking for where the access points were and where they'd stocked the streams with trout.

One of the perks of fishing and hunting is knowing that the money spent on the license goes directly toward giving sportsmen something to do and creating a robust ecosystem. There are always quibbles—no one trusts the game warden, and it's a ripe scenario for armchair quarterbacking, but as I see it, the proceeds from fishing licenses are spent to stock streams and brooks with tens of thousands of trout. Not only do the trout enhance the health of the waters, they also get people out onto the rivers, making the rivers valuable. If no one wants to fish in a river, history shows that it is soon used as a dump for whatever needs getting rid of. Of course, there are those who would care about the despoiling of a creek just because it is a creek, and a few would protest it, but none as loudly as those who want to throw a line into it. Fishermen have an intimate relationship with the water they fish.

I found some spots: Wappingers Creek, which flows just north of me, is stocked with thousands of brown trout and a few thousand rainbows, too.

First, I was going to go fish with Rory. Or so I thought. Rory is tall and exceedingly Irish—red haired, often with a bushy beard. I was amazed when I first met him at how ready he seemed to occupy the shared space of a Venn diagram on which one side said "swaggering ruffian" and the other said "finely tuned artisan." Rarely do you meet a man solidly in the overlap of those two circles, and I appreciate it. I still see this in him, but we've become closer and whenever you get to really know someone, they get blurry and hard to talk about.

I think the very reason that we became good friends explains a lot about Rory. When I called him to ask if he'd be a part of some aspect of a tour I was making to support *Chasing the White Dog*—I wanted him to be a part of an event—he decided that he should simply go with me for as much of it as he could.

Seriously? I mean, yeah, I'd love it, but don't you have things to do?

"Of course I do. But when am I going to have the chance to do this?"

So he came along, and we flew on planes together and stayed in hotels and gave each other the crooked eyebrow when the crazies showed up, and came to really know and like each other. He's game, up for more or less whatever comes at him. He puts up a front that would have you believe he wouldn't be at home at an art opening, but I know he went to art school at Parsons in New York. It's the same front that leads people to believe that he works at the distillery where he is, in fact, the owner. He doesn't actively try to impress people he meets. To the contrary, he waits for the product of his enthusiasms to prove what needs to be proved. The only thing I've ever seen him be fully ready to reveal his knowledge about is his tomato garden, which yielded a thousand pounds of tomatoes in 2012.

Our fishing trip began badly when the aluminum tube that held my fly rod didn't show up at the baggage claim in Grand Junction, Colorado. That was a bit of a heart-break, losing my father's rod, but I've got other things to pass along to West (some well-worn Sabatier knives, for instance, which are much more poignantly a Watman heirloom). The loss of the rod set the tenor for the trip. Even though Rory had plenty of fly setups I could use, we weren't destined to fish.

Our plan was to put Rory's drift boat into the Colorado, but the river was blown out—muddy from rains upriver— which meant the fishing wouldn't be any good. We drove up to the Roaring Fork, thinking we'd put in on the Fry-ingpan River, but every time we got near a launch to give it a go, lightning would crack overhead and we'd have a five-minute discussion about whether or not we wanted to sit in an aluminum boat on a river in a lightning storm. To his credit, Rory left it up to me. I'd come a long way to fish, after all, and he's the sort of guy who will go ahead and try to cheat death if you tell him that it's really important to you. I couldn't get close to convincing myself it was a good idea.

We did manage one ridiculous bit of fishing.

We spent the night at a luxurious, Xanadu-like lodge on ranch land the size of a state park. (Finally, my dream of North Dakota was delivered, for there I found myself in front of big fires, surrounded by taxidermy.) We were there to fill seats at a dinner that the chef was filming—when the cameras are rolling and the chef is talking about the coffee-crusted filet mignon and it's time for the shot where the people seated at the table smile and look excited, it doesn't play well if the seats aren't full. The chef is a friend of Rory's, and we had a great time. The next morning, we bounced down a ranch road to a pair of ponds that were stocked with trout.

The fish were huge—the size of my arm—and floating lazily near the surface. "Stocked" is an understatement.

These ponds were jammed with trout. Hungry trout. We were standing against a clear blue sky, casting shadows over the water, and we'd driven up in a loud truck. The trout should have hid. A normal trout would never bite whatever showed up next, but when Rory tossed a fly onto the water, four or five of them leapt to it. These trout needed something to eat. They were overcrowded and underfed.

I got some tips on my cast.

"Do you hear it snap sometimes?"

I did.

"You're pulling it forward too fast. Watch it; turn your body to the side and watch the back cast and keep it slow and steady."

I did as I was told, happy to be practicing my cast in one of the most beautiful spots I've ever been, standing in front of a bucket full of fish.

The ranch is in the canyons, which are the middle step up out of the western Colorado desert, before you get into the high-mountain aspen country that is the Continental Divide. The dirt is rocky and pale khaki brown, and the grass is sparse. The short hills rise quickly and top off with monadnocks of rock. It smells wonderful out there, piney and clear. There were no roads except the ranch road we'd driven up on, just a rutty gravel path, really. There were no power lines. There were barely any signs of people at all. Ten minutes back the way we'd come, there'd been a broken-down cabin.

I pulled in a fish—a mammoth rainbow trout, pale on the belly with dark spots across his golden back and a soft blush on the gills. The watercolor stripe on their sides can be orange, but these were faded pink, almost the color of the flesh of an apple right under the skin. His eyes were clear, the irises golden and the pupils large and intelligent seeming. It was fun because of the lesson and the scenery, but it wasn't really fishing. There was no secret being unlocked here, just hungry fish. There was no sport, either. This wasn't what I wanted.

Robert Altman said, in an *Esquire* interview in 2004, "I love fishing. You put that line in the water and you don't know what's on the other end. Your imagination is under there." I don't know what kind of fisherman Altman was, and it seems to me that what he said applies more tidily to pelagic fishing than it does to the trout stream—although trout streams are full of mystery and imagination as well.

Clearly, standing by the side of a shallow pond overcrowded with hungry trout, I had not imagined much, and I had not engaged with any sort of mystery at all. It occurred to me, however, that if I were a meat fisherman, if I were looking for fish to eat, I'd have found the perfect scenario. This was, far too literally, like shooting fish in a barrel.

I love to eat fish, but I began to understand that I wasn't after food.

If you live in a place where the waters are unpolluted (there aren't many left) and the fish are plentiful (there aren't many of those spots, either), you have a good shot at gathering food from the water. Unfortunately, I don't live in such a place. Man has yanked fish out of the water as fast as we have hurled poisons into it. The end of fish is not a faraway ship on the horizon; it has arrived.

Once I started paying attention to the reasons I might *not* want to eat certain fish—either because they are overfished or because they are polluted—I was soon left with a very short menu. Those big bluefish we pulled out of the waters off of Block Island were jammed full of PCBs and mercury and dioxin. New York State tells us that women beyond childbearing years and men can eat striper once a month, but kids and old folks shouldn't eat any. (Same goes for the striper we caught off the coast of Block Island. Striper has been well managed and are back in record numbers, but they are highly contaminated.) One meal a month? How poisonous must something be if a grown man can only eat it once a month? Forget it. Skip it. Skip the tuna, skip the swordfish, skip the marlins. Don't eat the caviar, the imported barramundi, the Chilean sea bass, or cod. Don't eat mahi you didn't catch yourself, snappers, roughy, shad, or shark. Don't eat farmed shrimp from Asia or king crab from Russia, and don't eat yellowtail, albacore, bigeye, or even tilapia unless it was grown in the United States.

(I'd blow all of this off for a chance to sit at Jiro's sushi counter in Tokyo.)

What's left? Maine lobster, if they manage it well. Oysters, scallops, clams, and blue crabs. Even the crabs out of the Hudson—and Russell caught 170 of them during the summer of 2011—are good to eat if you remove the tomalley, because crabs process all toxicity right there in their hepatopancreas.

I'll keep on fishing. I'll replace the fly rod and I'll catch and release, because the activity itself is worth it. But unless I'm standing on the banks of a river in Alaska, or throwing a line in the Florida Keys and pulling up mahimahi, I'm not fishing for food. Fishing for food is over.

CHAPTER EIGHT

The Marriage of Heaven and Hell

'VE CAST EVERYTHING I'D DONE up to this point in the best possible light, but the truth is that the project—my pursuit of real food—was starting to wear on me. Even fishing, my childhood darling, had betrayed me. My chickens were dead. My cheese wasn't what I wanted it to be. I'd bought a steer I could barely keep track of and was not ready to receive.

What had I done? I'd gone out looking for purity and quality, simplicity and grace, and I hadn't found it. I felt defeated. I'd gone all askew. I wasn't having any fun.

Part of the problem is in the literature. I read and read, and everything I read made me fearful or suspicious or sad. I can criticize some of what I read, but that doesn't mean that I wasn't absorbing the information. This is like when you read a bunch of crackpot stuff on the Internet for fun, laughing at all the kooks. Yet the next time you watch the MTV music awards, you will find yourself thinking, way in the back of your head, that maybe it really *is* some sort of coded celebration run by the Illuminati. I can dismiss Jonathan Safran Foer's book *Eating Animals* by undermining his main trope, but I cannot undo having read it. (He asks, coyly, why we don't eat dogs. Predators don't eat predators. We eat prey. Dogs are predators. They hunt with us, and they make us better hunters. That's why we don't eat them.)* Other books—*Tomatoland*, for instance—are simply terrifying and inarguable. All this paranoia, all these rules and proscriptions filled my head. I had anxiety dreams about livestock—barns full of pigs crowded into tiny boxes, squealing. When Russell brought over a few crabs he'd caught in the Hudson, I couldn't decide if I believed that all the toxicity was in the tomalley, and I couldn't bring myself to eat them. (I've since been convinced.) I started acting more out of fear than love.

I believe in the existential satisfaction of the search, but I am a student of literature, and I know that to be on the *wrong* search is despair itself. The hunt did not make Ahab a better man. To get the search wrong is to fuck it all up.

William Blake was a complicated guy. He was a Romantic poet, groundbreaking engraver, and a visionary in the best and weirdest sense of the word—he was a visionary who *had visions*, and that's not usually what we mean. He wrote *The Marriage of Heaven and Hell* between 1790 and 1792, when the world was on fire. (England had very recently lost the American Revolution, and France was in turmoil. Heads would soon roll.) What he meant by marrying heaven and hell wasn't the marriage of punishment and reward. It was the marriage of Dionysian impulse with Apollonian wisdom. Dionysian impulse is creative; Apollo-

---

*There are cultures that *do* eat dogs. Mostly, it seems, dog meat is eaten in times of deprivation, or as a ritual. Different cultures have different ideas about what constitutes food, but in our dog-loving, man's-best-friend setup, we'd rather have a dog by our side than on our table.

nian thought is analytical. The two must be balanced, and my marriage was all imbalanced. I had replaced fishing with reading about which fish I shouldn't eat and pondering the degradation of the oceans that had led to the current state of depletion and pollution—not just at my desk, where such activity is acceptable, but at the fish counter. It's important—drastically so in this age—to approach a fish counter with knowledge of which oceanic fruits are better choices than others. It's also important not to have a small-scale nervous breakdown every time you want to make chowder.

I work in a little shed that I've renovated in the very back corner of our yard. When we bought this house, the little shed was in shambles. The floor was frost heaved and bent and splintered. The joists under it were rotted. The building was racked off of its foundation, twisted and no longer sitting on the blocks. The stud walls, however, were in great shape, as were the rafters. Ironically, I've heard it was once a chicken coop, about ten feet deep and fifteen feet long. When I was digging around, ripping up flooring and shoveling up the splinters of the floor joists, trying to figure out how to fix it, I found the big bones of large animals tucked away in the dirt, hip joints and shanks. My first thought upon discovering bleached bones under the floor was that I'd found Hoffa. I think they were beef bones, and I only wonder at why there were so few. It's as if someone spent five minutes butchering a steer in the back corner of the yard, or emptied a stockpot there once.

After some time spent with screw jacks, trying to lift the building up off the dirt myself and listening to the creak and sputter of a building on the verge of collapsing on top of me, I hired a contractor.

I love it out here in the shed. There are more than a thousand books, all in a state of disarray so profound that a visiting librarian would feel as if he were being bitten by ants. There are postcards pinned to the walls, memorabilia I've picked up here and there, and pictures that make me happy: Rachael holding West when he tucked his toes into the ocean for the first time, Jimi Hendrix playing guitar, a painting of horses ready to race that a friend of mine bought for me at the prison in Hull, England, where Philip Larkin worked. I sit happily, mostly, at a hundred-year-old farm table, with a nice—but properly curtailed—view of my yard, centered on a red wheelbarrow upon which not much really depends, if you get right down to it.

It's on the short list for my favorite room in the world—right up there with my kitchen, the Rose Reading Room at the New York Public Library, and a couple of rooms accessible only in my memory. But it gets lonely, and there's just no escaping the feeling that if you are sitting alone in a shed all day and much of the night, you might be going a little crazy. Have you ever tuned in to a radio station—one of the few stations that isn't canned—and listened to a DJ slip over the edge? He's alone at the decks, and no one cocks an eyebrow of warning when the jokes fall flat. He simply thinks that his audience is laughing right along with him. That's what I'm afraid of. One of my favorite antidotes has been to walk down the street to the pizza shop at the end of my block, get a slice, and say hello to George Stevenson, who is inevitably there, drinking tea with nine thousand sugars in it and chewing his way through a pack of gum. (He chews each piece maybe five times before he takes it out, stacks it up in a wad on the table before him, and unwraps a fresh one.)

George is a Vietnam veteran. He was, in his youth, a star

high school football player. I believe his record for pass
receptions in a single season still stands. He worked for
Con Edison for five years before he was drafted. He saw
horror in Vietnam. His friends died around him. About a
year after George got home, he had a stroke, which cost
him the use of his right arm and his right leg, and his ability to speak. He learned to walk in a lopsided gait. He also
learned to talk again, in short repetitive bursts. He can't
read (I don't mean he is illiterate. I mean his brain can't
turn letters into words).

George learned to use his left hand by painting. He
studied locally and then at the Art Students League in
New York City.

He carries a stack of Polaroid pictures in his shirt
pocket of paintings he wants to show you and often has
a photocopy of an article about himself or some piece of
his past he wants you to read. I own one of his paintings.
It has a mountain in the distance—Crow's Nest, across
the Hudson—and the foreground tilts terrifically forward,
flipping into a flat plane reminiscent of Howard Finster's
perspective-free pictures. In the middle of the painting
are three skunks, which he modeled after the three ply-
wood skunks that I put in my yard after I was sprayed
while taking out the trash. (Skunks are to our town what
rats are to the New York subway.)

Needless to say, I like walking half a block and saying hello to George, with his excellent mustache and his
always-worn kutte vest. He doesn't say much, but we are
friends. I like having a pizza shop to go to. I like taking
a break in the middle of the day and walking out of the
shed, where I sit, alone for hours, unsure of whether or not
I still understand the English language.

See me this day at the threshold of the pizza shop in

faded blue jeans, shifting my weight on the concrete with
my hands jammed into the pockets of my down vest, my
hair a mess, unable to think of a single thing I wanted
to eat.* Instead of making food better, I'd turned the entire
world into a nightmare of pink slime. A man who has
boxed himself out of a slice of pizza is a sad man. The
pizza shop is no place for high anxiety. I'd made some terrible mistakes.

When eating out, I had drifted into a weird indecisive-
ness, like an observant Jew forced into vegetarianism due
to the overwhelming lack of suitable kosher options. I
was now well versed on the wretched conditions of our
fisheries and the wretched conditions of the fish therein.
Steak frites made me think of concentrated feedlots, and
chicken in any form made me think of the slurry of filthy
water through which the carcasses of the recently slaughtered birds are run to "clean" them and "cool" them (air-
chilled birds are the way to go if you're buying chicken in
the market).

I had wanted to create a utopia, a way of eating that
erased anxiety, and I'd done exactly the opposite. Further-
more, my critical self seemed to have overtaken the creative part of me that wanted to have fun making food. The
deeper down the rabbit hole I fell, the more my analytical,
Apollonian impulses eclipsed my Dionysian impulses.

Pity the writer's wife, always talking her loved one down
off the ledge. (There ought to be a group, like Al-Anon,

---

*This seems to be an occupational hazard of a sort. I ran into a kid I know
who had become an organic farmer, and he told me a story of being
unable to eat potato chips. He wanted some, he bought them, he tasted
them, and they tasted terrible. "Seriously," he said, laughing, "I can't eat
chips anymore. That sucks."

where the spouses of writers can get together and discuss the experience.)

That's it. I'm done. Nothing works. I could always go to law school. Is it too late? (I don't know why law school is the fallback position of writers everywhere, but it seems to come up a lot at moments of despair. If you're visiting me and notice a catalogue from Yale Law on the coffee table, tread lightly, I beg of you.)

My failure, I felt at the time, was twofold. I had failed in my search, and in so doing, my work—this book—must also fail.

Rachael's been doing this for a while, though. She knows. She's like Dan Aykroyd playing Jimmy Carter in episode fifteen of the second season of *Saturday Night Live*. A kid calls in freaking out on LSD. Bill Murray, playing Walter Cronkite, tries to dismiss the call, but Aykroyd's Carter understands immediately. After Aykroyd/Carter figures out that the kid took something called "Orange Sunshine," he talks him down. "You're very high right now. You'll probably be that way for about five more hours. Try taking some vitamin B complex, vitamin C complex. If you have a beer go ahead and drink it. . . . Just remember you're a living organism on this planet and you're very safe. You've just taken a heavy drug. Just relax, stay inside and listen to some music. Do you have any Allman Brothers?"

Rachael knows the difference between a pretense of despair and the real thing. The first—which comes up all the time when I start talking about how I don't understand what it is I'm supposed to be writing about—is easily dismissed with "You say this every time," a wifely roll of the eyes, and a smile. I might sputter about how it's different this time, but I know already that it isn't.

She knows when I am serious. I told her how I had broken everything. I wanted to walk away from the book, the idea, the whole thing. We talked for hours. She expertly steered the conversation toward all that was working. This year, our home garden was booming. I had become enraptured by the idea of subterranean irrigation systems, and figured out that I could bury a drainage pipe—nothing but a four-inch, black plastic tube, corrugated and perforated—to collect water when the soil was saturated and seep it back into the ground as it dried. I built a raised bed, with a higher tier in the middle for tomatoes, and lifted one end of the pipe out of the earth so I could water directly into the soil. We had eight-foot-tall tomato plants, we'd only had to water the garden twice,* and we had none of the mildew or rot that comes with our wet summers. The chard and the kale had been plentiful and strong. We'd grown potatoes in funny little bags like totes, which you fill up with dirt and whatever it is you want to grow. I'd thought that getting the potatoes out of them might be easier than digging them up. Actually, it was harder (where is a good spot to dump a few gallons of dirt out onto the yard?), but the bags are cool, for sure, and the potatoes were great. Weren't we, she indicated, at that very moment sipping gimlets made from a lime cordial I had made myself? Hadn't we been eating in a different way, after all? And hadn't it been fun?

So we weren't going to subsist on fish I'd caught on my own line a short walk from our house, but what about the bacon I'd cured from a locally grown pig? I'd salted, sugared, and peppered a slab of belly meat, and after it was firm to the touch, I'd hung it. I sliced it and hot smoked it,

---

*Rachael claims that she watered it a few times, as well. So, okay, maybe four times total all summer.

or fried it for BLTs. What about those BLTs? They were summer poetry, with lettuce from the CSA and our own fat, juicy Brandywine tomatoes.

She was right. I had been running all these sidelines, but I hadn't been thinking about them. I hadn't been thinking about the way the CSA had changed our eating. I hadn't been thinking about the terrines of pheasant that I'd made from the birds I brought back from Dakota, struck through with pistachios and nice chunks of pork fat, layered with a breast of pheasant in the middle.

I had analyzed food so heavily that I'd lost touch with what eating is about.

I have an intense memory for the food I've eaten. I remember meals. Rachael says I remember every meal I've ever eaten, and that's not true, but I don't forget the good ones. They are the waypoints of my life. I could list meals I liked for hours. I could cook most of them, reverse engineering from memory the aromas that came into play.*

I remember the squid ink orecchiette with octopus and roasted garlic at Pesce in Washington DC on what was my first assignment as a food writer in the summer of 1998. It was thick and the octopus was toothsome and meaty, the garlic was deeply caramelized, and everything in the dish had been miraculously cooked to the same texture and swirled in thick, black ink. Rachael and I laughed at our black teeth and joked that it was a good thing it wasn't our

---

*There is a special section in my memory for meals I've eaten and liked that I could not re-create by simply trying. I don't eat a lot of molecular gastronomy; it doesn't interest me, and that's not what I mean. I mean, rather, that I really don't understand how they make the honey-roasted pork shoulder at Yeah Shanghai, or how they managed to get the saltwater eel inside of the baby napa cabbage at Toraya and have them both cook perfectly.

first date. Watching someone eat a big plate of black food isn't a winning sight unless you are already in love.

I remember the lamb ragu on gnocchi at Lupa a couple of years later. I can put myself by the banks of the Rappahannock River with a small gang of friends the day after my wedding. We had a case of white Graves that was rosepetal floral and mineral clean, and two and a half bushels of plump, fat oysters left over from the wedding, wonderfully cold after a night buried in ice. Some of them were the size of my palm. A couple of them were the size of my whole hand.

I can bring to mind the streets of Chinatown in Manhattan, where a woman with a folding table on the sidewalk sold me small sandwiches of sautéed greens drizzled in sesame oil, spiked with garlic, and wrapped in a soft white bun. Jamie Nicoll, the owner of Summerfield Farm (which was one of the first farms to be written down on a menu in America), once cooked me pigeon he'd aged in the crisper for a week after shooting it out of the rafters of his barn. It was deep, gamey, fat from cracked corn. There was the aforementioned wood duck that Russell had shot and I'd smoked, eaten off the cutting board in the middle of Rachael's fortieth birthday party. I remember the subtle mousse of sole, served in an eggshell and topped with caviar at Le Pavillon in Washington DC, when I was twelve years old. The bouillabaisse we ate at that first big dinner party in Richmond. The steaks I cooked with my dad on a grill set on cinder blocks over a wood fire out on Long Island. The bushel of crabs that we'd caught at a friend's house out on the Eastern Shore, when Rachael and I had just gotten together, and she pretended she didn't know how to crack a crab so I would do it for her. I was alone in

Paris when I ate at Au Pied de Cochon. I ordered the tête de veau and wondered, briefly, if my wretched French had failed me and I was about to confront an entire head—I'd have dug in, of course, but I was nervous for the patrons around me, forced to watch a man alone at a table eating a head. The fried tomatoes that Rachael and I ate on the banks of Lake Erie, wondering what to do with our lives. The fish tacos I ate out of a paper bag while watching a women's surfing competition at Huntington Beach, wondering why I didn't live in California. The time I served my friends a plate with little rosettes of beef in a circle, the first one raw, the second one bresaola I'd cured myself. ("Well, I guess I'd always known it would come to this," said one of the guests.)

I'd wanted my food to be "better." But I didn't know what better was going to be. I didn't know where I'd end up. I didn't start with "Food would be better if it all came from within a hundred miles of my house," or "I won't eat any meat I haven't killed myself." This wasn't "Max eats roadkill for a year!" or "We're only going to eat cats because there are too many cats." I just wanted the food to be better. How could it be better? It's always been excellent—whether it was a sloppy barbecue sandwich in Georgia or a rack of ribs out of my smoker on July Fourth. It is the way I know where I was, who I was with, and who I was at each moment of my life. Hadn't I come to another chapter? Hadn't I drawn a line in the sand, inserted a page break, and changed the way we ate?

I thought about what I had wanted from this book, and I thought about the way I'd talked to people about it.

A common reaction was for them to say something about the English food writer and farm-to-table advocate

Hugh Fearnley-Whittingstall. Or, more dramatically even, "I love stuff like that; I loved the books the Nearings wrote about going back to the land."

Those people, the Nearings, the Fearnley-Whittingstalls, are great inspirations, but what I'd really wanted was something that *didn't* take you back to the land. You don't have to walk out of the city and buy a farm—and you'd better not even try to, unless you have a magically refreshing bank account and a television show all lined up about doing it. I like what I do. Rachael likes her work. We like our town, our proximity to New York City, and the school that West goes to. I just wanted to do what I could with what I had, tune the system up and get better at it. I wanted my readers to think to themselves that maybe they should make their own bacon, despite the fact that they live in a tiny apartment in a city. I don't want a Garden of Eden, something out of reach, something aspirational. I want to do things that everyone can do. To turn myself on to the seasonal, agricultural rhythms. To live, in other words, as if I were on a farm but without the farm.

I wanted a pizza. So I made one.

I bought four glass jars of Ronnybrook milk, pasteurized but not homogenized. I added citric acid and rennet, and once I got a clean break, I heated the curds, mixed in salt, and strained them in a colander lined with cheesecloth. Then I turned them out into a bowl and pressed them. I worked them into a ball and then heated it up in hot water. I kneaded the ball and stretched it like taffy and pressed it some more, repeating the process until the cheese turned shiny and silky. It was bright white, chewy, and milky and sweet. Fresh mozzarella.

I made a slowly fermented dough, basically but not exactly Jim Lahey's no-knead pizza dough. It was the

first in a series of experiments to give bread back to
Rachael. She's discovered, like many people, that the reason her stomach hurt for years is that she doesn't digest
gluten well. I'd read about a study in Italy where people
with certain gluten intolerances found that bread that
had been properly fermented did not distress them. The
theory is that a long, slow fermentation of bread dough
breaks down the protein chains that some people have a
hard time digesting. So far, so good. Since I started making pizza and loaves this way—the experiments are in
their adolescence—Rachael has not experienced an iota
of pain.*

On the stovetop bubbled a simple sauce of our own
tomatoes. I laid firebricks in the oven and let them get hot
for an hour and a half before I slid the first pizza off the
peel and into the hearth.

When West, Rachael, and I sat down to eat that night,
we ate a pizza with cheese I'd made, sauce I'd grown, and
crust I'd baked. It was fantastic: charred and chewy, a perfect marriage of bright sauce and luscious cheese.

John Whiteside had said to me that his customers had
wanted something different. "People are realizing that you
really can control your life, but you have to be an active
participant."

Of course, failure was going to be a part of this, I realized. So what. Like Samuel Beckett wrote in *Worstward
Ho*, "Ever tried. Ever failed. . . . Fail again. Fail better."

It is clear to me that a person who makes bread by hand
knows more about bread than a person who uses a bread
machine, even if their success rate isn't as good. I would

---

* Gluten intolerance is often idiopathic. Just because this works for Rachael
doesn't mean it will work for someone else.

add a layer to that as well and suggest that a person who makes bread by hand has available to him knowledge about food in general that he wouldn't have otherwise. Once you begin looking at processes, once you begin thinking about ingredients and techniques, once you know how to look at *one* thing carefully, you are simply better at looking.

CHAPTER NINE

From a Crooked Angle

I**T'S AN EASY TRUTH THAT** when we travel, we eat—we
might look at art, or sit by the ocean, or walk in gardens, but because we are away from home, we must search
out our food, and because we are away from home, that
food will be different from our own. I suppose there are
those who, when traveling, seek out the comforts of home
from the get-go—foolish French girls searching for *pain
au chocolat* in Georgia, unable to accept grits; timid business travelers darting past the brasseries of Paris to shoot
into the Marriott and wolf down a wedge of iceberg and a
burger. (There is a place for this activity, of course, about
ten days into the trip, when one starts chafing at being
forced to feed from the same trough day in and day out.
This is the instinct that drove me to search out lo mein
and egg rolls in Milan on the night before Rachael and I
flew home—it was a terrible rendition, but we slurped our
greasy noodles with gusto, *sic semper tyrannis*.)

Because I am food obsessed, I think a lot about where
the meals are coming from when traveling, and whether
or not they will fulfill whatever expectations I have, whatever level I feel I must rise to. Eating in New Orleans is a

more tense and thought-out affair than eating in Regent, North Dakota. In New Orleans, you dare not waste a meal; just filling in the slots on the calendar can be challenging arithmetic. In North Dakota, if you don't have anything you've shot on hand, you simply reach for the thick steaks from the excellent butcher shop in Dickinson and char them on the kettle grill while the prairie wind whips the charcoal into a fury that will compete, barely, with the rapidly dropping temperatures of dusk.

A person could have a good time making a list of the degrees of food pressure in various places. The Geoculinary Advisory System (GAS) would be a simple color chart, like the one Homeland Security drummed up to keep us on the lookout for terrorists:

- Green/Low: You're in a place with little regional food of interest, utterly devoid of tradition or activity. Keep driving.

- Blue/Guarded: You might find something if you're lucky.

- Yellow/Elevated: Interesting foodways are available, and there's either a local crop or fauna that is worthy of note, or a scene where people are eating well. Pay attention.

- Orange/High: The waters or fields are rife with produce of varying kinds. People here pay attention to what they eat, and it's a vibrant scene, with newcomers adding to the mix.

- Red/Severe: You're in one of the central, distinctive food areas in the world. If there were a Slow Food version of UNESCO, this place would be registered. The GAS equivalent of three Michelin stars: worth a trip just to eat there.

Although I spend a lot of time on the road, I don't like travel. I don't find a language barrier exhilarating—it's thrilling only because of the level of work involved. If it takes half an hour to agree that the building is very tall, or to explain what a gargoyle is, it *feels* as if something great has been accomplished, as if you've successfully navigated an intense point of philosophy. But you haven't. You've only successfully navigated the simplest imaginable conversation. (This is why people fall in love in foreign countries, I think, because the intensity of dialogue *feels* as if it is profound, even when it's not.) Nor do I feel that I'm a better, smarter person because I've gone out to breakfast in Florence. If anything, I feel like a mark, played by a massive industrial-tourism con. But I can't deny that travel induces a state of wakefulness. We attend to things when we travel, which is one reason we like it. Pico Iyer wrote, in his famous paean to roaming titled "Why We Travel," that the great joy in it is in "seeing everything I thought I knew in a different light, and from a crooked angle."

When I started thinking about foraging, I didn't think of it as a correlative experience. I didn't connect the dots and come to see that learning to forage was like traveling—that is, being aware and awake to what is around you, and seeing things differently. To the contrary, when I thought of foraging, I thought of mushrooms and weeds.

In the spring of 2012, I took West to a park in a nearby town for a walk-and-talk led by a local woman who promised that we could forage edible and medicinal plants along the paths. She led a troop of us, stopping here and there to point at a plant and say it was "good for you." Sometimes the plants were "very good for you." Occasionally, they'd be "good for your blood" or something similar. It was all very vague, and never delicious, and the level of expertise seemed reminiscent of, perhaps, what you might hear if you asked a primary-school art instructor about the recipe for Titian's pigments. We were deep in the Wise Woman woods, a holistic approach to health that would, I'm pretty sure, leave a lot of folks dying of pneumonia and typhoid if it were adopted in any real way. To each their own, I suppose.

West learned to munch on dandelion flowers, which led to a pretty hilarious few weeks of him plucking them and taking vigorous bites. He looked great with little yellow petals flecked on his lips. (There aren't any poisonous look-alikes, only some bitterness in the dandelion itself and a couple of plants that are even more bitter when they briefly look like dandelions in the spring.) I warned him not to eat dandelions in public parks or at school, since they would no doubt be covered in some dreadful chemical. Our yard's plentiful dandelions, I promised him, were 100 percent organic.

The walk-and-talk was underwhelming, to say the least, but the lesson that West took away from it was invaluable. He was seeing what he had once known in a different light: he was looking at dandelions differently. He hadn't traveled very far at all—one town to the north—but when he came back, the nature of our yard had changed.

I had thought of foraging as a speciality, a hobby for the gastro-fringe, but I came to see that to take up foraging, in whatever manner, is to learn to travel in your own place. For foraging, really, is only being alive to where you are. Where once there were weeds, there might be food, and they will look different when you see them that way. What's more, I came to see foraging in a broader light, closer to the dictionary definition of the word. Foraging is searching widely for food.

In Richmond, right before we moved to New York, when I still had my last restaurant job, we were with my parents scouring a Russian deli in the far reaches of the suburbs, because it was close to a Vietnamese market we liked, and if the Watman family can find an exacta like that—a Russian deli and a Vietnamese market within forty yards of each other—it's a safe bet you'll find us there. The deli was full of the usual stuff—smoked fish, bags of blini mix—and then, in the cooler, something caught my eye. I dismissed it at first. If memory serves, I even walked out of the shop, hovered on the curb, and told my parents and Rachael I needed to duck back in.

There, nestled in the ice, was a seven-ounce tin of sevruga. This was at the height of the black-market caviar trade, when the sturgeon were being overfished and fish eggs were being confiscated by the ton at the airports in New York. I didn't know that at the time.* I'd returned to double-check the price.

The woman behind the counter was full-on Muscovite. Glamorous, hair-sprayed like a drag queen, tight clothes, animal prints.

How much is that caviar? I asked.

"Twenty-seven dollars," she said thickly.

Can you get a lot of it?

"You want how many?"

Seven?

"Yes. I have. Next week Tuesday."

I went back, and sure enough, she had them for me. I'd spread the word among restaurant folks. I sold the tins for seventy bucks—half of what the retail price was at the

---

*A couple of years after we'd left Richmond, I read an article about the huge smuggled shipments of caviar that were being seized, and the vigorous black market in fish eggs. Amazingly, it was written by a woman I later met, after she'd moved on to writing about the illegal trade in Virginia's unlicensed moonshine. We had a great time comparing notes over sandwiches in Virginia.

time. No one was disappointed. Most folks wanted more, as soon as I could get it. I flipped caviar for a month or so, doing about three drops and eating all the profits. I would pay for the purchase of seven by selling three—I think once I sold five of them under duress—and I'd keep the rest. Over the course of the month, Rachael and I and our friends ate about seventy ounces of caviar. For those of you who are bad at math, that's an average of two and one-third ounces a day. Every day. Having caviar on hand like that changes everything. What was once dainty and sacred—it comes with little spoons and tiny dishes; it is the closest food gets to cocaine—became hedonistic and plentiful. For one glorious month, I was Scarface with my nose buried in a mountain of caviar. I know what it is to smear half an ounce of caviar across a bagel and cream cheese in the morning (it's great). I know what it's like to stuff an omelette full of caviar as if it were no more costly than button mushrooms. I know what it's like to coat big plates of fettucini with caviar and cream.

Why didn't everyone know about this trick? I've thought about it a lot over the years—of course I have; I was smearing caviar on bagels—and it has come to remind me of a walk in the woods I took with my old friend, the photographer Jim Bartlett. We were young, living in a college town. He was small and quick, habitually dressed in army surplus, blue jeans, and granny glasses, with short, black hair. Now he goes to wars to take pictures. He always had a military/survivalist bent. For Jim, the shit was always about to go down. It was just a part of how he lived. You had to know, as far as Jim was concerned, how to tap out your own rounds for a .357. He was young and bright and fairly well off, but something about the world struck him as profoundly dangerous. We worked at a farm together for a spell, and we would drive out there in his little Mazda pickup with stickers on the tailgate in the shape of bullet holes, drinking quarts of Gatorade against last night's debauchery. We decided, one pleasant afternoon after our duties were complete, to have a stroll out by where we'd seen a fox at a windbreak. Jim started pointing things out.

"If you are in the woods, and you have to spend the night . . ."

Jim, I said, laughing, *why would that happen? What do you mean?*

"You're in the woods now, right? What if we got lost? What if I broke my ankle, and I had to spend the night while you went for help?"

I wasn't convinced, but he seemed excited to tell me things, and I was interested in what he was saying. He pointed at felled trees—trees blown over by the wind or hit by lightning—that were still connected to the stump. One of these could easily form the ridge beam of a makeshift shelter. You gather something leafy and thick—laurel, for instance—and lean it against the trunk of the tree to create an ad hoc place to sleep, affording some shelter from the elements. Then Jim started pointing out what I could eat: fiddleheads, lamb's-quarter, plantain, dandelions.

You have to know some things, yes; you have to know what lamb's-quarter looks like, or what caviar is supposed to cost. But really, all we are talking about is keeping your eyes open.

When I met an exciting, eccentric bartender named Nick Strangeway in New Orleans, we hit it off. He's an interesting guy, to say the least. Thin and urbane, Nick has gained some serious renown as a cutting-edge drinks crafter, and a bit of a goofy reputation for growing enormous beards, although he'd just shaved. At dinner, he ordered two espressos. He carefully told the waitress that he didn't want a double espresso. He wanted two single espressos. I've never seen anyone do this, and I've never seen anyone express their instructions so carefully, with such an intense mixture of kindness and forcefulness. There is no messing up what Nick asks you for. When he tells you what he wants, I imagine you move compelled to bring it to him, as if bewitched.

He forages in London, where he lives. He told me how much he loves to walk to work—stolen time, basically, during which he is not responsible for anything. One day, he saw a small stand of trees bearing fruit in an industrial neighborhood, a blighted place by a canal, but there were the trees. He moved fast and got his staff out there to harvest the fruit, which they brought back to the bar and made drinks with.

René Redzepi, the wild culture chef at Noma, three times as of this writing voted the best restaurant in the *world* (impossible to eat there, impossible to get a reservation, impossible to afford, never mind that it's in Copenhagen for crying out loud), has the right idea. It's not enough that you find it outside. It should bring something to the table. We should *want* to eat it—the way West wants to eat dandelions.

This is the mind-set that I brought to Block Island on our yearly beach trip to that lovely, bucolic place. For the two years prior, I'd obsessively clammed. You can dig quahogs out of the sand if you buy a license, and they are delicious. The natural population of quahogs was fished out of the sand years ago, but the Block Island Shellfish Commission seeds about 100,000 clams into the water every year. In 2004, the commission sold 1,738 licenses. The little shop by the harbor master's office sells clam rakes. It's all good fun, and for the two years prior to this year's trip, I had engaged enthusiastically in the difficult work of digging the delicious little things.

This last year, however, I had something else in mind. It started with salt.

There are a lot of reasons to go to the beach, but a large portion of the pleasure derived from the ocean is that it's salty. You can float in the water. The air seems to have texture. It makes all your little bumps and bruises and cuts heal quickly. And the food you eat there—nothing stokes the passions of the palate quite as hot as the seashore—is brackish. Brought to the seashore, folks start pining for brine. They want oysters, they want fish, they want buckets of crabs and rafts of fried clams. They are not wrong.

Why not get to the heart of the matter? Why not see if I could harvest the ocean itself? What could be more guttural, more intrinsically oceanic than the ocean's salt? When at the seashore, one wants to eat of the ocean. Why not simply try to eat the *ocean*?

I arrived at a rocky beach with a lobster pot. I was wearing jeans because I hadn't actually thought about how deep into the water one would have to walk to fill up a lobster pot. So I turned to Russell, who was wearing a bathing suit and a wet-suit shirt. (It's become a joke between us, the things I ask him to do. Somehow it's always his job to walk into the water, or to stab the lobsters, or to do whatever bit of work I am conveniently not prepared for.)

He reported to me later that his daughter, the five-year-old Jacqueline, asked why they had to make salt, clearly thinking of all the salt shakers she'd seen. I believe his answer was along the lines of "because Max told us to."

Russell's wife, Candace, and I lugged the heavy pot of water back to the truck and bungeed down the lid. I went bouncing down the dirt roads, hoping that I didn't spill all of the water on my way. (Everything can change: I hadn't thought that I'd have to get wet to get the water, and I hadn't thought about how bumpy the dirt road to the beach was, and I hadn't really thought about how heavy a lobster pot full of seawater is when you have to carry it for seventy yards.)

I filtered the water through a cheesecloth in a colander and set the pot on the stove to simmer. It was slow going, but over the course of a couple of days, water evaporated and I began to see, when the water was reduced by about a third, little blossoms of salt crystals floating on the top. There was sludgy salt at the bottom, too, which I scooped out and put in a baking pan to put out in the sun. There it was, I thought. I had gathered maybe three tablespoons, and I wasn't sure if I'd get any more. Was that really it? I was pleased as I could be to see that I'd gotten some salt, but it didn't seem right. Ah, well—I am a man accustomed to weirdly underwhelming victories. They are the house specialty.

With two or three inches of water left in the pot, I turned it off overnight and left it on the stove. The next morning I was amazed. The entire bottom of the pot was covered in a thick, white sludge. Could it be?

It was.

I carefully poured off what was left of the water and tasted the clotted crystals that remained. It was clean, and bright white, and it was salt. Some of it had crystallized into big flakes. Overall, it was chunky and slightly wet, like sel gris. I got about a cup and a half. It tastes gentle and pure, with a nice crunch and a calm, salty brine flavor more like Maldon than like the French salts.

I was overjoyed, and I was motivated. People often cook lobsters in seawater, but does anyone cook with it as an ingredient? I decided I wanted to. I had dipped my finger into the seawater while it reduced. It was delicious. I wanted to make seawater risotto.

I'd invited our friends over to dinner on Wednesday and had hoped to have a fish to cook, but our fishing trip had been delayed due to weather, and a new menu began to take shape. Then it began to consume me.

I wanted to try the sea snails again. I'd foraged some the previous year and cooked them with butter and garlic. They'd been all right, but I knew they could be better. Periwinkles are not native to America, but they are numerous on any northeastern rocky shore. They are small, and their shells are striated green and black and gray and classically spiraled to a high point. The inside of the shell is white, and sometimes seaweed green will edge the lip. It is thought that they came to these shores clinging to the bottoms of ships, or clinging to the rock ballasts, and multiplied. They climb all over the rocks wherever there are little pools that remain after the waves wash out. If you find one, you are bound to find a thousand. I gathered them with the kids—*You guys are low to the ground, so you can see them better!* West and Jacqueline designed a periwinkle farm, with a little barn and a bit of wet sand they fenced in with other rocks. We had a few dozen snails in no time.

I set these on the counter in some strained seawater,

thinking that like a carp, if they didn't eat for a day and had nothing but clean water to hang around in, they might not have any grit when we ate them.

While the snails crawled all over one another in a pan on the kitchen counter, I wrote down the menu:

PERIWINKLE FRITTERS

SEAWATER RISOTTO

FISH WITH ANISE-INFUSED SALT

It looked like a good start, but it was very . . . white. Where were the vegetables?

I was on a roll: There was seaweed everywhere. Some of it must be edible. I quickly Googled what seaweeds were fun to eat—what brave new world is this?—and finally came upon bladderwrack. This is the ubiquitous plant with the little pods that help it float. You've seen it. Everyone has seen it. It brushes up against you and feels slimy and stiff in the water, and it's everywhere. So the dish became seawater risotto with bladderwrack.

Since our fishing trip was delayed, I had to buy the fish, a disappointment in a meal that had quickly become a sort of vacation-at-Noma foraging extravaganza, but there was nothing to be done about it. I found some good, firm cod at the fish shop. It was from nearby, they promised, and although I don't trust teenagers working in fish shops in touristy places, I figured the airport on Block Island was probably too small to fly much fish into, and it did seem like good fish.

I was set.

I took a small scoop—a couple of tablespoons—of my new salt and spread it on a cookie sheet. This I placed in a low oven and splashed with Ricard—an anise-flavored spirit, like Pernod (and, in fact, made by the same company). You could use either one, or ouzo, or sambuca, or absinthe. I stirred the salt once the Ricard had evaporated, splashed in some more, and stirred it up again. I repeated this process until the salt was a sort of pale yellow-green and tasted like anise. Then I put the salt in a teacup, ready for the plating.

I rinsed the bladderwrack and then soaked it for an hour in fresh water (as opposed to salt water). I trimmed the heavy stems, leaving the tenderest leaves and the bladders arrayed on a sheet pan. (I was probably overly cautious in my trimming, because I didn't know if it would be any good.) I roasted it in a slow oven at 275°. It turned slimy, like okra, and then it crisped and browned. It was full of big umami flavors and tasted littoral, like urchin.

I walked into the water myself and slurped two quarts of seawater into a big Mason jar. As I walked back to the truck, a man walking to the beach with his family said, "Didja get your moonshine?" I pondered this for hours. It seems almost certain that he simply saw a guy with a ratty straw hat carrying a Mason jar of clear liquid and said the first joke that came to mind, but it stuck and I decided it was a good omen.

I boiled the periwinkles briefly in their shells and then set to plucking them out. It is tedious work. You have to get past the little door they close on the world, a tiny disk of shell. Then you pluck them out with a toothpick, skewer, or small knife. It goes on forever, and your pile of meat never seems to get any bigger. But it will end, and they are flavorful. I recommend that you eat one every once in a while just to keep your spirits up. For the fritters, I made a simple beer batter: beer, flour, and a beaten egg. You can separate the eggs and beat the whites, and I probably should have, but I was tired from picking the winkles out of their shells and running late for the same reason, so I didn't. I sprinkled Spanish smoked paprika and Block Island Sel into the batter and mixed in the snails.

Seawater became a vegetable stock with the addition of a couple of tomatoes, an onion, and celery tops. I added hot stock to hot rice gradually, tasting it all the while, afraid of it growing too salty. It came just up to the edge, and I finished with two cups of fresh water so as not to go too far.

I made daiquiris for everyone, and we gathered on the deck while the sun streamed across the trees. It was the golden hour (that short window when the light is perfect and you should take pictures) and the violet hour (which separates the day from the night with a drink) wonderfully arriving at the same moment. I cut scallions into the fritter batter and fried the fritters flat, like the clam fritters from Maryland that I love so much. I sprinkled them with a little Block Island Sel, and we ate them with our hands. (West and Jacqueline loved them, knowing that they'd had a hand in it, but the other kids couldn't be tempted.) The pictures I have of the dinner—the first part, anyway, before we all got down to eating and the sun set—show everyone laughing, holding little fritters in their hands, drinking rum or crisp white wine, and they make me want to go on vacation again, right now.

The risotto was brilliant. In a lifetime of cooking, it is the dish of which I am most proud. The crunchy, roasted umami depth of the seaweed, which I drifted over the top of the rice, was the perfect counterpoint to the wild seawater flavor. The dish was perfectly balanced and totally new.

The anise salt on the cod was gentle and just right.

It had taken days and leaps of inspiration to get this

meal done, but I got it across, and I was surrounded by
smiling faces at the table, laughing and digging in. I don't
even think they noticed that they were eating things that
they generally disregarded. Snails? Seaweed? Salt water?
There's an outdoor shower at your beach house to get rid
of what I put on those plates. But I'd seen them from a
crooked angle.

Patience Gray wrote in *Honey from a Weed* that foraging was the example par excellence of the time spent gathering and preparing being all out of balance with the time
it takes to consume the food—and in fact, she was talking
about snails. She knew that the time spent gathering them
was enjoyable and that the time spent preparing them was
equally so (despite it being so long). In her understanding
of foraging, there was always an anxiety about whether or
not snails were the only protein available. If we don't rely
upon these calories, however, this is pure pleasure. This is
the topsy-turvy world of luxurious toil. Who doesn't want
to watch kids construct a periwinkle farm on a rocky seashore? Who doesn't want to laugh over a glass of bracing
white wine while chewing through rice plumped with the
ocean? Who doesn't want to take home from the beach the
very essence of why you went there, to stick it in the cup-
board and sprinkle a bit of vacation on the plate throughout the rest of the year?

CHAPTER TEN

Bubbles Gets the Gun

O F COURSE, VACATION IS JUST THAT. It *isn't* the rest of the year, by definition. The rest of the year, and then some, most likely, would be filled with beef. My steer had grown to harvest weight, and his time had come.

Yellow Tag 879—aka Bubbles—met his quick end on an August day, in an aluminum horse trailer parked on the gravel driveway of Shawn's meat-processing plant, which is behind a big brick house with formal white columns set atop a perfect Virginia hill. The plant is called Hidden Pines Meat Processing, and Shawn's business is mostly deer. He and his team process about 2,500 deer when the season is on, 60 an hour sometimes. The plant is set low, in a small hollow, a cluster of utilitarian buildings around a gravel lot in which a redbone coonhound and a blue heeler wander, looking for pats on the head. There's a barn and two cold rooms and a concrete floor with a big drain under a porch roof. The tools and the Multivac machines are in the cold room to the left. There's Metro shelving with latex gloves and vacu-bags, files and labels, and a little satellite radio. There are sharp knives, bone scrapers, and a floor-standing band saw that cuts through thick bones with a high squeal. Shawn's two meat grinders stand on the floor and are the size of refrigerators, although not quite as tall. He sunk $30,000 into them. It's clear that they would grind your arm into meat before you could pull it out. You'd hear only the *chunk* of the bone being snapped.

Even a cursory look around the plant was enough to assure me that I would never have been able to butcher Bubbles myself. At a one-day class on butchering pigs in the back of the Mountain Restaurant Supply shop, in Newburgh, New York—part of Jennifer Claire's series of food-education classes—I was one of thirty-odd students who walked past the showroom full of plates and spatulas, past the wall of gleaming knives, through the room with the chef's coats, and gathered in the small show kitchen in the back. With the exception of a couple of eager hunters in the front of the class in Realtree camouflage zip-up sweatshirts, and a middle-aged couple who looked as if they'd arrived on a Harley, the class could have been mistaken for a film studies seminar at New York University. In front of me, a tweedy fellow with a bit of a stammer took notes on his iPad. Thirty of us had skipped Sunday brunch to prop ourselves on stools and little wooden chairs in this dark, cool room and watch Mark Elia butcher a pig.

The pig had been split and stretched out on the stainless steel under the fluorescents. This was no suckling; this hog had been long and fat, and if its head had still been attached, it would have been equal in length to an average man. The head was also halved and skinned, resting to the side with a rough, slightly bloody appearance, as if it had been worked over with a pruning saw.

Elia wasted no time. He assessed the animal with affectionate expertise, his hands moving over the meat, evaluating it. He looked hungry—not from lack of food but from lust, as a good cook should. He asked for a volunteer from the audience, and a thin young woman with dark bangs popped out of her seat. She pulled an apron over her charcoal-on-black downtown sweater set and grabbed the meat saw excitedly.

Elia instructed her on how to separate the ham (which is the entire back leg of the hog) from the carcass.

"Let the saw do the work," he said. "Cut right there, at the second rib bone."

She took a firm grip on the ham, placed her saw in between two ribs, and started down. She smiled as she pulled back smoothly and the tight teeth of the sharp saw began to sink in.

"That's right; always start on the back stroke," said Elia. "When you feel yourself get through the bone, stop."

She worked with fluent, confident strokes and within moments, the raspy sound of the teeth across the bone faded, and the ham sagged away from the trunk of the pig.

"Whoa," said the young woman. I was impressed and a little startled by the depth of her response: she was utterly absorbed, slightly breathless, and seemingly full of butter-flies, as if she'd just fallen in love. She was without irony or posture, totally unguarded. "That was *so* cool."*

---

*We learned to further butcher a whole ham, separating it into cuts more familiar in beef: top round, eye round, and bottom round—cuts that are immensely useful (small roasts that they are) and that are rarely seen in the store. (One simply follows the seams of fat—imagine a slice of spiral-cut holiday ham and the way the slice is really a few pieces that come apart naturally. Those are seams in the meat, and each of those pieces is a slice of a roast.) We learned that muscles that get used a lot need slow, moist heat, while muscles that don't should be cooked fast and dry. We learned that there's a gland in the fat of a Boston butt (the top half of the front leg), about forty-five degrees off the bladebone, which one

The saw she used wouldn't have been long enough to cut through the rear quarter of a steer. It's the difference between chopping down a fruit tree in your yard and being a lumberjack.

Shawn is in his mid-thirties, born and raised in Madison County. He's happy, and it shows. He runs a serious farming operation when it isn't deer season. He does what he loves, and he is proud to be doing it for himself.

Steve Lamb, John Whiteside's only full-time employee, had driven the steer over on the trailer, with his daughter—twelve, I'd guess—in the truck with him. The steer poked his head out between the aluminum railings, sniffing the air. This was different, yes; this was not an open field. He was alone for probably the first time in his life, but he didn't seem overly worried. (It's impossible to judge the mood of animals in any subtle way. When I wrote about horse racing, I realized that the key to our interaction with animals is that they don't talk. We do what we can to guess. Although cattle farmers will disagree, I would suggest that cows are not especially expressive. With horses, you can see small variations, levels of nervousness and little instant reactions to everything around them. Cows are slower. Both get nervous: I had watched, only the day before, as Steve moved a herd of cattle across Graves Mill Road. Every one of them stopped at the double yellow line

---

should cut out because it creates an off flavor. (It's a little yellow wad, about the size of a tablespoon, and it's been removed from some of the butts one can buy, but not all of them.) Elia showed us the ribs and how to cut good scaloppine off of the leg. I was surprised that there are shell steaks and hanger steaks on a pig. They're too small to ever show up in a butcher case, but they are delicious. (These are classic butcher cuts, it turns out, or, more deviously, boot cuts, because butchers sometimes slip them down into their boots and walk out with them, knowing that they will just end up ground into sausage.)

in the middle, looked down at it, and got tense about it. Most of them jumped over it as if it might be a river or a tree—very horselike behavior, but not bright. My steer might have been that nervous.)

Steve was leaning against an old Toyota truck, cradling a tidy bolt-action .17-caliber rifle. Shawn took the rifle—"It never misses from twelve inches," he said—and walked toward the trailer. Things were moving forward. I was full of wonder at what was about to happen and how I was about to feel, my blood racing, my nerves on edge. Not so the tween girl, who smiled and said, "Nighty night."

This caught me off guard. Aren't tween girls supposed to be the most deeply empathetic creatures on the planet? Shouldn't she have been asking questions about why we had to kill this animal and promising that she'd never eat another hamburger as long as she lived?

I didn't talk to her. I felt it wouldn't have been appropriate, although I regret that feeling now. I might have if I hadn't been so nerved up, and so surprised at seeing her there, and so intimidated by the men around me who were so practiced and casual with the death of the largest animal I'd ever seen die. She had the country-girl steel. She didn't question this process or have any time for existential questions about the future of the herds—ours, the steers. She must have known that if this didn't happen, her dad wouldn't work. She knew that without this death, the herd couldn't continue. I don't know how many slaughters she'd attended, but I know that she'd grown up farming, where death is a part of the equation. All that I expected to be troubled by, she accepted.

There is no such thing as a wild herd of cows. We care for them, we raise them, we protect and feed them because we eat them. We get to live on the food provided

by the herd, and the herd gets to live because the food
they provide is valuable, which is why we have cows.

Shawn got in the trailer, and the steer swung his big
head over to look at him.

The steer's tongue reached out to the rifle and gave it
a friendly, exploratory lick. He'd never met a human who
didn't feed him. He didn't know that the tide had turned.

There was a pop, and the steer fell over sideways, finished instantly, his legs shaking through the haywire sig-
nals that the nervous system sent through his big body. He
trembled and shook for probably twenty seconds. It felt
like ten minutes to me—ten minutes of the trailer bucking
and shaking on its wheels, crunching the gravel, skittering. Then it stopped.

It was through, the steer was dead, that was that. Shawn
and Steve opened the back door of the horse trailer, hooked
a heavy chain around one of the steer's back legs, and
hoisted him into the air with a forklift attached to the front
of a big John Deere. The steer hung and twisted slightly
on the chain—twisting in the wind, as is said—his free
leg jerking reflexively. A body as big as that takes a while
to really shut down, and muscles would still be twitching
when he was fully skinned and gutted. A thing alive parts
with life roughly, slowly.

With a sharp six-inch Victorinox boning knife, Shawn
cut a quick slash in the steer's neck, opening up three or
four inches at the jugular vein. Frothy red blood spilled
onto the gravel in a gush. Cows have a little over four gallons of blood, enough to fill a lobster pot. Shawn looked at
his blade and shook his head. He likes to cut fast enough
that his blade remains clean, but the knife was shiny red.
It took about fifteen minutes, maybe twenty, for the steer
to bleed out.

The dogs were very attentive to this action, but they kept their distance.

The hide was still dirty, crusted in manure and mud and stuck with flecks of grass and field dirt, and after the animal had bled out, Steve drove the John Deere over to the concrete patch of floor in front of the cold room, and Shawn carefully hosed the carcass down. Then the work began in earnest.

Shawn sharpened the knives quickly, after every few cuts, and moved with precise, knowledgeable confidence.

How'd you learn to do that? I asked.

"I used to watch my grandfather. I guess I just picked it up."

Shawn cut incisions through the gambrel, what we would call the Achilles tendon, and slipped big steel hooks through the cuts to hold up the legs at chest height. (It is interesting that the gambrel refers not only to the hock but also to the tool a butcher uses to hang the animal by the hocks. That kind of linguistic correlation implies that we're talking about a practice we've been doing for a very, very long time.) He cut the hide around the rear hocks and began by peeling the hide downward from the back hooves. He sliced connective tissue and the hide sagged down like an old rolled-over sock with no elastic left.

Shawn worked steadily down the carcass until the haunches were nude and then asked me if I wanted the oxtail, which I did. He skinned it out and left it connected, cut around the anus and the penis, and lifted the carcass higher. Shawn worked steadily, deftly, downward, revealing the animal's subcutaneous layer of wet yellow fat. He made cuts, leaving the hide whole but slicing it expertly so it would come off of the frame. Two big flaps angled down on either side of the brisket, the chest of the animal, to the armpits.

This is perhaps the strangest moment, visually, of the process. From the waist down (toward the sky on an animal hanging from the gambrel) what you see is meat—huge chunks of meat still on the bone, cloaked in a layer of fat that never makes it to the butcher counter, but recognizable. From the waist up, toward the concrete floor, you are still looking at a dead animal.

I came to suspect, then and there, that some strategies of butchering—hanging the animal upside down, covering the animal with its own skin as it is removed—have to do with simply coping with being the first step in the binary setup that Claude Lévi-Strauss defined as being between what is found in nature and what is found in culture—that is, the raw and the cooked. Lévi-Strauss is famously hard to unpack (and fraught and unreliable), but I think his theory about this is useful, in the way that Freud's theories remain at least artistically and poetically relevant to the way we think about our minds. My own understanding of the raw-and-cooked theory is that the raw is that which exists with us, in nature, and the cooked is that which we have manipulated by our culture so that we can consume it. Even the foods that we eat without cooking—steak tartare and sushi, for example—are expertly manipulated. They are "raw" in that they have not been heated, but expert knife work and artful presentation have moved them well beyond the raw state. We don't rip flesh out of the natural world and eat it. We might as well, if we did, just eat one another, and that distinction—not eating one another, not viewing people as meat—is important to the vast majority of humans. Less dramatically, it is inher-

ently difficult to eat something you've cared for. You need
to distinguish between the pets and the product, between
the animals you were patting on the head and feeding,
and the animals that are feeding you. For many animals,
the transformation to meat is immediate. Consider Hemingway's hyena in the *Green Hills of Africa*, which he
shot badly. (Hemingway tries to blame this on the hyena
by mentioning that it was running when shot.) The hyena
circled "madly, snapping and tearing at himself until he
pulled his own intestines out, and then stood there, jerking them out and eating with relish." Clearly, the hyena
has no need for a cultural distinction between the raw and
the cooked.

For us, however, the process of transformation, the first
step—killing, skinning, cutting—is the biggest. It's more
of a leap than a step.

I think it is clear to everyone that we have hidden the
raw too well and removed ourselves from the sense that
there is a state of nature at all, or that the animals that end
up cooked are a part of the natural world we share with
them. (The existence of ships full of live sheep, 75,000 at a
time, sailing out of Australia seems like evidence enough
by itself.) Here, in a tight Virginia hollow with a couple
of dogs lazing in the sun, the raw had not been shunted
away. The leap from raw to cooked, from natural to cultural, from walking to consumable was brilliantly clear.

Shawn worked until the hide hung like a cape, and then
he cut off the head and threw the hide and the head in a
fifty-five-gallon trash bin.*

---

*The bin was marked with the Valley Proteins logo and the word *inedible*.
Valley Proteins is a rendering plant, which means that Shawn sells all
of his "inedible" by-products to be converted into proteins, probably for
feed. I can't imagine that I could have raised a reasonable complaint

One long slice down the belly revealed the guts, all clinging together like a bunch of tomatoes on the vine. The colors of guts are amazing: pink and gray-white, bright blood-red and maroon. Steve's daughter angled herself for a better look. We saved the liver and the heart; the rest flopped out into a big tray and was disposed of in the rendering can. Shawn hosed down the inside of the animal.

An electric reciprocating saw cut the spinal column and cleaved the carcass gently into two halves. Shawn then started a cut at the twelfth rib, which separates the quarters, and grabbed hooks to hold up the bottom quarters while Steve made the final cut with a saw. Shawn rocked back on his heels, his tremendous arms fully flexed, muscles popping like an ad for whey protein, and took the weight of the whole quarter, which must have been two hundred pounds, at least. He walked the quarter, holding it by the hooks, resting it against his apron, to the cooling rack in the big cold room, where he hung it up.

Shawn's cold room is a living room–sized walk-in. My quarters hung there, alone, hooked on a stainless-steel rack. Arrayed thusly, the transformation was complete. An hour and a half ago, an animal had licked the barrel of a gun; now hundreds of pounds of raw meat hung from hooks in a chilly room.

The quarters would hang for four weeks, twice as long as Shawn hangs them, longer than the industry standard, but good for the development of flavorful, tender meat. It

against Shawn's little bit of money on the side, even if it means that this animal protein will be ground up and fed to chickens. It does give me some insight into the lack of available hide processing: I'd asked if we could process the hide, but we didn't have anywhere to send it. If it'd been deer season, we might have had some luck, but as it stood, there was no one around who knew a tanner.

cost me seven dollars a day to run the air conditioner for the two extra weeks. I'd lose some yield to evaporation, and they'd have to trim more of the external fat off the carcass when it came time to butcher the quarters, but it'd be worth it.

Grass-fed beef is famously leaner than grain fed, and leaner meat is generally tougher. The enzymatic breakdown that would take place over the extra two weeks would tenderize the meat and add deeper flavor.

FOUR WEEKS LATER, I was back. Shawn brought in a remarkably taciturn man to help with breaking down the quarters. They'd cut off the dried, deeply purple-brown crust that had formed over the meat during the hanging, and they were ready to go when I arrived.

They started with the rib end of the animal, sectioning out the chuck and the rib loin.

It's almost impossible to understand how beef is sectioned unless you have a map, so I asked my friend, illustrator and editor Katherine Messenger, to draw me one.

Throughout, I felt like an old man on a safari, pointing at things the hunters should shoot—not really helping, not really hindering, more or less unnecessary but obeyed, regardless, on account of the fact that I was footing the bill.

Their butchering worked for me because, mostly, I wanted the cuts to be big. I wanted the tenderloins separate and intact. (I don't like those double steaks, T-bone and porterhouse, and so on. They have a big reputation, but it seems crystal clear to me that the tenderloin and the rib loin are totally different cuts of meat, which want different treatments and different cooking times, and to combine them is to put yourself in a position where you must compromise by cooking one of them slightly better than the other.) I wanted the chuck in seven-pound slices I could smoke for barbecue. (This was a risky experiment. I wanted to try smoking shoulder, which has become the choice cut for barbecue in Texas, edging out the classic brisket. But the shoulder clod is a forty-pound cut of meat. I have very little call for forty-pound cuts of meat. I'm not saying it would *never* come up; I just figured that if I had a few seven-pound cuts, I might make barbecue more often. So we sliced right across the whole chuck.) I wanted all the loin steaks, rib and short loin, sliced thick and on the bone. I wanted my sirloin steaks thick. I wanted the eye of round whole so I could cure it in salt and make the outstanding, ruby-red, juniper-scented charcuterie called bresaola. I wanted my briskets with the fatty deckle cut still attached. (This pointed top—top as it's lying in the butcher's case, anyway—is often disastrously trimmed off of the brisket, which makes an already-difficult cut to cook nearly impossible.)

"How thick you want these?" they'd ask, and I'd hold up my fingers, always about 1.5 to 2 inches apart.

The work was fast, and the meat piled up around the room. There were white tubs that collected trim—all the little bits and pieces that you have to cut off the primal cuts to make things the shape they need to be. I had expected to be overwhelmed with the amount of meat, but as it was sectioned, it became sort of manageable. Fourteen rib steaks is a lot of rib steak, to be sure, especially if each of them is thick and weighs about a pound and a half. But fourteen rib steaks is not an unimaginable amount of food. You can eat fourteen steaks.*

The entire haul was vacuum packed and frozen: I had 366 pounds of beef (slightly less than I'd thought I'd get). Surprisingly, 160-odd pounds of the meat turned out to be ground beef. Back at Graves Mill Farm, we ate rib steaks that very night—they were delicious. (As I've worked with the beef, I've come to the conclusion that it wants a little more age—and I'm setting up yet another refrigerator in the basement to do just that. I'll also use it to cure the bresaola I'll make from the eye round.)

The next day we fired up Nathan's big Texas smoker to smoke one of the big slices of chuck. We held it at three hundred degrees for six hours, after giving it a rub of salt and pepper and a light sprinkling of granulated garlic. Despite logging hundreds upon hundreds of hours of barbecue between us—Nathan runs a part-time catering business as a side project, and I have been serious about barbecue for years—neither of us had ever smoked anything from the shoulder. We were working, basically, with a cut that does not exist. We followed our instincts, kept it simple, and let the white oak do its work.

---

*I learned later that Shawn claimed that this meat was the only butchering job he'd ever done that made him hungry. According to Nathan, he put off the cleanup to go eat.

It was perfect. The different cuts that are in the chuck produced a varied barbecue, some of it flavorful and chewy, some of it mind-blowingly tender, all of it a tremendous success.

"I think that's the best meat that has ever come off of my smoker," said Nathan as we stood around the island in his kitchen with Shannon and sliced and nibbled until an embarrassing amount of what had been a seven-pound slice of beef was gone, eaten by only three of us. We were in a heavy protein, meat-drunk haze.

Back home, Rachael and West and I ate chili and burgers and steak. West was excited—still is—and would ask every time if what we were eating was Bubbles.

"Wait. So this is Bubbles?"

The first time he asked, I anticipated disaster, but I wasn't going to lie to him. I told him it was.

"Wow," he said, stabbing another forkful. "It's great."

Rachael said, "Wow, you know what? Bubbles is really good. The meat tastes . . . more."

She hit the nail on the head. There is a vapidity to the flavor of supermarket beef. It has become simply a protein. In the words of Gertrude Stein in *Everybody's Autobiography*, there is no longer any *there* there. This meat was more.

When Nathan headed toward the slaughtering of the few lambs he raises on Graves Mill—the small subsistence-farming project that he continues for himself—I arranged to trade, pound for pound, lamb for beef. I'd thought, perhaps, that I might find a pig farmer, too, and see if I could work something out there, but already, the beef felt precious to me.

Nathan gave me some interesting advice along those lines.

"Use it as a resource," he suggested. "It's valuable, and

a lot of people will understand that. I traded a leg of lamb for a week at a beach house."

All told, I'd spent approximately $1,300 on 366 pounds of beef: $3.55 a pound. That's big box–store, ground-beef cheap, and I'd gotten every single cut. It was a good deal. It took hustle, and it took time, but I have a freezer brimming with beautiful meat. I know where it came from, and I know how well the animal was raised. I saw him walk the pasture, and I saw him die. I won't have to hover above a meat case for a very long time. I've removed myself from one of the most violent, disgusting, and disheartening processes industrial farming has delivered.

I had not, in the end, had anywhere near as much of a hands-on experience with the raising of the steer as I'd wanted. I'd intended to care for him myself. But that was only part of the experiment. I knew this animal. I knew why he died and how.

In the April 8, 1974, issue of *Newsweek*, there was an article about the diarist and photographer Peter Beard. He'd brought out a book with Alistair Graham called *Eyelids of Morning*, which was about the crocodiles that lived in Lake Rudolf (now known as Lake Turkana) in Kenya. The crocodile population was large and dangerous, and the lake was terrible country, and the two men had lived there and suffered all sorts of mishaps along the lines of those suffered by men who go too far into strange countries. It's a fantastic book. I loved it as a child because of the crazy pictures—these weren't the vanilla pictures one finds in books for kids about animals. Rather, these were actual crocodiles, some of them dead, and actual victims of crocodiles, some of them also dead. There were drawings of monsters and pictures of gorgeous people. I forgot about it for years, rediscovered it recently, and love it still.

Beard was obssessed—I think he still is—with the incompatibility of man and animals. Uncontrolled, with no management, the animals will all die; it is the nature of the way that we grow into places. We will leave them nothing. We will take the lion's share of available resources, and the animals will starve while rummaging through our trash. "Do-gooder conservationists have done the most harm," says Beard in the *Newsweek* article. "None of them are interested in pictures beyond Joy Adamson French-kissing milk into her lion cub's mouth. The whole emphasis is on one sentimental animal, rather than on the protection of the entire species."

The easiest way to ensure that a species will be protected is to make sure that it is worth something to humans.

The death of Yellow Tag 879—along with the other steer that were harvested that year at Wolf Creek Farm— created the value that allows his herd to continue. What's more, the Wolf Creek herd is an organic machine that maintains a huge swath of paradisal Virginia farmland. Because of the pressure on land like that, even now, if it weren't farmed it would be something else. Without a man who wants meat, there would be no herd. Without a herd, there would be no pasture.

Water, grass, and the herd, all rolling along together, are stewarded by the hard work of John Whiteside and Steve Lamb. I pull beef from my freezer without queasy hesitation. This beef is a victory.

CHAPTER ELEVEN

Harvest

And yet this time removed was summer's time;
The teeming autumn, big with rich increase.

—*William Shakespeare, Sonnet 97*

H ISTORICALLY, RACHAEL HITS THE WALL on seasonal produce about two weeks before I do. She chafes, in
other words, a mere two weeks into asparagus season—
a season so specific that in England, they have an *official*
start date (Saint George's Day, April 23) and an official
end date (Midsummer Day, June 24).* We don't have such
rules, of course, but I feel about eating asparagus in July
as others feel about wearing seersucker after Labor Day.
So when it hits, we eat it. I like it chopped and slightly
overcooked in simmering chicken stock, then tossed with
olive oil and Pecorino cheese and orecchiette. I like it
grilled, and in risotto. Mostly, however, I love thin stalks
blanched very briefly in salted water and served room
temperature with a squeeze of lemon, a drizzle of olive oil,

*It should be noted, out of fairness, that there are some seasons she
would extend indefinitely if she could wave Demeter's wand and change
the way things grow: she'd eat real tomatoes every day of the year, as she
would oysters. Oysters you can do, seeing as how they've transplanted
a bunch of southern oysters up north to where the water is never warm
enough to think that it's a month without an *r* at the end. Tomatoes,
forget it.

and flakes of good salt. Always eat asparagus with your fingers, because even the strictest book of manners will say that you can and because it is great, sexy fun. Sadly, after fourteen days of blanched asparagus and funny-smelling pee, Rachael will start to rebel. About fifteen years ago, I started making a case for seasonal indulgence, which was how I'd come to think of it. When there's corn, you overdo it. You eat it until you can't stand the sight of it. When there are tomatoes, you eat them every day in big salads with basil and on transcendent BLTs. You don't eat them the rest of the year because . . . well, because they are crap. Who wants a BLT made out of a pale, tasteless winter tomato?

Isn't it great, I'd muse, my fingers covered in olive oil, gesturing with a bright green stalk of asparagus as if I were about to call the orchestra to attention, *how you just eat it and eat it and eat it until you can't stand it anymore? Then it's gone. It's totally gone. You don't get any for another whole year. We'll be totally sick of this by the end of the season, and next year we'll be jumping out of the gate to get it again.*

But the harvest comes on strong. Suddenly, if you've gardened very well at all and if your CSA was worth the price of admission, you will have far more food than you can eat. At first, I hadn't really thought about it. I just grew sick of eating kale all the time, and I began blanching and freezing it, knowing that I'd love it in February, when I hadn't seen any chlorophyll in as long as I could remember. *But, Max*, I thought, *aren't you doing exactly what you don't want to do? Aren't you setting up a system by which you'll be eating kale when it is no longer in season?*

Nancy Singleton Hachisu wrote in her book *Japanese*

Farm Food about meeting her husband in Japan: "I couldn't understand why Takaaki would bring me so many of one kind of vegetable when he came to visit. Later, I found out why. When you have a lot of something, you eat it at every meal. You don't choose the vegetables, they choose you. My education was a slow process, and I was typically stubborn. It took me many years to wean myself off of planning a meal around recipes. Or even from planning meals ahead."

With a serious garden and ever-increasing shares from my CSA, eating everything we grew became a challenge. Full-immersion seasonality is very fulfilling (although as Gabrielle Hamilton pointed out while writing about the incessant eggplant season in Puglia, it can be trying if it's too limited). Throughout the summer, we always had a little bit of something else and a comfortable knowledge that most of the fruits of harvest would end, that our plentitude was temporary, and that asparagus season or tomato season was short-lived.

However, the teething increase that is early autumn is not the same kind of beast. It's hard to imagine getting sick of soft-shell crabs, for instance, since their season is so short. Unless you've got a molting tank like the one that chef Jimmy Sneed built out in Urbanna, Virginia, so he could have soft-shells all the time (in which case, please get in touch), it's not as if you're going to be staring at a pile of soft-shell crabs, wondering how you could possibly eat them all. In early fall, however, one confronts, for instance, turnips. They are all harvested at once, basically, maybe over a couple of weeks, and suddenly there's a pile of turnips like you're a turnip salesman, like your counter is the produce section of a supermarket. To eat them all would be seasonal eating as practiced in a gulag. You must find things to do with them.

The hardest part of the harvest, I think, is that it is easy to be tired of it all. It's just like when you shoot something and it's lying there dead and now you must deal. There is little difference between plucking and gutting a shot bird and canning forty-five pounds of tomatoes. The thrilling act, the heroic moment, has passed. Now it's just knives and toil.

The curse of the big harvest—a huge pile of food—is also its blessing, but you must figure out what to do with it all. It stops being about eating with the season. The real goal, I began to see, was to preserve the overabundance, to have it later in the cold, chlorophyll-deprived season.

That's how a mountain of turnips became a gallon of kimchi. If you read a little about kimchi, that spicy and remarkably hip pickle that is the mainstay of Korean eating, you quickly learn that it is made not just from cabbage but from nearly everything. Sandor Ellix Katz—the author of the monumental *The Art of Fermentation*—has gone so far as to blur the border between sauerkraut and kimchi. He calls what he makes kraut-chi, and he has whittled the "recipe" down to "Chop, Salt, Pack, Wait." He doesn't measure his salt, and he doesn't exclude—as far as I can tell—any vegetable at all. It's very encouraging. And one needs a bit of encouragement. For while I'm no stranger to fermentation, this bit of controlled rot in a container in my kitchen set me slightly on edge. There was no distillation step, which guarantees that whatever bacteria have shown up would be dead and left behind while you pulled off only the beautiful ethanol that the ferment had made. Nor was there a flood of yummy, beneficial bacteria to rely upon as there is when you introduce the starter cultures to begin cheese. This was simply packing stuff into a jar and letting it sit around for a long time and then *eating it*. Things can go wrong, of course, but the process is designed to welcome certain bacteria, and as with cheese, the key thing to know is that beneficial bacteria will win out over pathogenic bacteria if you create an environment that favors the former. The other key thing is to not eat things that don't strike you as edible. Truly ruined, rotten things are not an acquired taste. Kimchi might be strong, sauerkraut might be complicated, but nothing edible presents as inedible. (Durian fruit? Maybe. I'd also not argue with anyone who said that they figured lutefisk was best left untouched.)

One of the most powerful bits of Katz's book comes in his defense of amateur fermenters in response to Paul Stamets, who writes that "making Kombucha under nonsterile conditions becomes, in a sense, a biological form of Russian Roulette." Katz replies, "The idea that kombucha (or any ferment) is safe only in the hands of technical experts denies the long lineages of home and village production that spawned them and plays right into the disempowering cult of specialization. Make sure you understand the parameters of the selective environment you need to create, and you are not playing Russian Roulette. Basic information and awareness are important. Empowered with them, you may ferment without fear."

I got a daikon and chopped it up with CSA bok choy and turnips that were never going to be eaten before they wilted and rotted. I mixed them with salt and a little bit of sugar. The next afternoon, they were surrounded by their own water in enough brine to cover them very well. I chopped a dozen cloves of garlic and added about three tablespoons of chopped ginger. I used to hate peeling ginger until I realized that if I chopped off big hunks of the skin, I could use that later to make ginger syrup. So now I just basically square off the ginger. Typically I am a big fan of the Italian way of chopping as opposed to the more exacting French technique. The names for certain chops—julienne being perhaps the most commonly known—are in French because they developed stringent standards and measurements for how things should be chopped. The Italians, on the other hand, tend to simply cut things; and if some of the onions melt away into the sauce while others remain recognizable, all the better. Still, when you are chopping raw garlic and raw ginger, it's a good time to think like a Frenchman. A big hunk of garlic will scrunch up the face of even the heartiest eater.

I drained the vegetables (I think this is the way in which sauerkraut and kimchi differ) and mixed up a new brine of salt, a little more sugar, a lot of crushed Korean red pepper (half a cup or so), fish sauce, and a little soy. I sliced a bunch of scallions and mixed them in, then mixed all of that—the brined vegetables, the garlic, the ginger, the scallions, the new brine—together well and packed it in a jar. Right away—I tasted it immediately—I could tell I was on to something. This stuff was bursting, leaping with flavor.

Over time, the kimchi got funkier, melded together, and settled into tasting like it should. I had left out dried shrimp because I didn't have any, and the fermented chile paste because I had run out of it after having had it in my fridge for an aeon, but what I'd made tasted like kimchi. Excellent kimchi.

It only got better. I finished off the last of the first batch on a bowl of rice with some furikake (the Japanese seaweed-and-bonito rice flavoring) sprinkled on top at my desk for lunch. It was months after I'd made it. The first hard frost of the year had blackened all my ferns, but I was eating my harvest. The kimchi had a slow, satisfy-ing chile-pepper burn and a slightly sweet undertone. (I made a note to use less sugar, if any.) It was still crunchy and vibrant, with big, fresh flavors of ginger and garlic. It had completely transformed into a unified food, the way a stew moves from individual aromas in proximity to one another and fuses into a dish.

At the community garden up the hill, the patches seemed to fall into neglect around Labor Day. No one seemed to care anymore about the last tomatoes (although some of those folks had a lot of tomatoes left on the vine, being pecked by birds and sucked on by bugs). No one wanted any more leafy greens. Things got weedy and overgrown.

Perhaps they were all disheartened by the wave of leaf rot that hit every tomato plant up on that hill. All of our leaves yellowed, then browned, then fell off. All of our stalks got crinkly and deathly ill. My plants had developed a truly amazing fruit set. There were paste tomatoes every-where, but I lost about half of them because the plants weren't strong enough to hold on to the fruit. By picking the tomatoes early—at the first blush of ripeness—I pulled a little over sixty pounds of tomatoes. I lost more on the counter at home. Some weren't healthy or strong enough and rotted before they ripened. Twelve pounds went into sauces eaten right away on pizzas and pastas. Forty-eight pounds were canned.

I hadn't canned since my jar of cornichons, and never by myself. Canning made me even more nervous than fermenting. Fermenting, after all, even if it's just rotting on the counter, is working with the natural proclivities of salt and bacteria. Also, in my experience, a ferment gone wrong is an obvious thing. Canning, however, is an attempt to create an environment in which nature *can't happen*. Kafka once wrote, in Aphorism 52, "In the fight between you and the world, back the world." Indeed. It seems improbable, if not impossible, that a thinking person would simply put some jars in boiling water and imagine that after so doing he could go ahead and set those jars on a shelf in the basement and everything would be fine. It works, obviously; it just doesn't feel like it should, and it certainly didn't feel like it should the first time I did it.

Canning got easier as I went along, and I grew confident in the process. I found that my *mise en place* was important. I'd gather the tools then double-check the list. I'd clean it all, lay it out in an orderly fashion, and then triple-check. Lots of people like to have big all-day canning parties, but I find the work tedious, and I found that I liked doing only as much as I could process in one go. I even split the process into two days.

On the first day, I made a lot of sauce—familar territory to say the least. People can whole tomatoes, but I don't like the taste of tomato seeds, and I like smooth tomato sauce.

I blanched the tomatoes in big batches—twenty pounds at a time in the biggest pot I have—after cleaning them up a bit and cutting out the stems. Then I set a china cap—a cheap colander shaped like a cone with little holes in it—over a one-gallon Lexan tub and first smashed the tomatoes through it by using a big wooden pestle, then squished them around with a spatula. Some of the tomatoes needed help popping open, even after all the boiling and squashing, but a paring knife made quick work of that. Once halved, the tomato is defenseless. The tomatoes in the Lexan were the consistency of tomato juice, and the seeds, skins, and errant stems were left in the china cap. I put the tub in the fridge.

On the second day, I put the tomato juice on the stove and heated it up to a simmer. I wanted to cook it, reduce it, and purify it.

While that cooked—unseasoned, so far—I brought water to a boil in the canning pot, rolled the temperature back a little so it was a calm boil, not a leaping-out-of-the-pot-and-trying-to-become-a-gas type of a boil, and I lowered my pint jars into the pot. In a small saucepan, I heated the lids. You need, when canning, to have everything you start with hot so you don't have to account for the amount of time it takes to heat up. You aren't actually presterilizing, though lots of literature will say that you are. The sterilization happens in the canning process itself. It's just that if you were to start with cold glass and cold tomatoes and cold lids, you'd never know when they were truly hot, and for how long they had been that way, and if any pockets of unheated material remained.

Once I had everything hot and the tomato juice had reduced to the consistency of a thin sauce, I started bottling it. Processing only one jar at a time so nothing cools down, you first spoon in a quarter teaspoon of citric acid to make an even more uncomfortable environment for bacteria. (You can use lemon juice, and I think with certain tomatoes you needn't add anything at all, but since tomatoes are right on the line—lower-acidity foods must be canned under pressure—it's a classic case of better safe than sorry. Better just to add a little bump of acidity to lower the pH.) I ladled sauce into the jar, topped it with a new lid, and finger tightened the band. One at a time, I lowered the full jars into the water bath. Once they were all filled and submerged, I covered the pot and cranked the heat. The kitchen was steamy and wet; the jars stayed in for forty-five minutes. I then lifted the jars out of the water bath, careful not to tilt them, and put them on a towel to cool. One at a time they popped while they cooled in a draftless corner. One after the other, *pop*, and then twenty minutes later, *pop*, as the pressure changed and the lids sank. The test, the next day, is the same one you use at the store to make sure that the jar of pickles you are buying is properly sealed. If the lid moves when you press it down, the jar isn't sealed.

In batches of eight jars at a time, I grew a cool shelf in the basement of bright, red tomato sauce. It tastes wonderful, and it'll last almost until I harvest more.

The first time I canned sauce (and every time thereafter), I had a little sauce left over that wouldn't fill a jar. Rachael was out of town, and I invited Russell, Candace, and Jacqueline over for an early pizza experiment. Heavily hydrated no-knead dough became tomato-and-cheese calzones for the kids. They loved them. We made pizzas in the oven, with firebricks on the oven rack that I'd heated for an hour and a half at five hundred degrees. The pizzas were long, flimsy things on the peel, but they had a great oven spring, and I cranked the broiler to char them nicely on the top. We put Fontina and duck pastrami from Cochon Butcher on one, brussels sprouts and Benton's bacon on another, wild boar salami and Parmesan on a third, and pure mozzarella and tomato on the last. Candace asked what I had done to make such delicious tomato sauce.

Russell cut me off, jumping in and laughing: "He's going to say he started by growing the tomatoes."

He was right.

"But what else? What did you put in it?"

I put almost nothing in tomato sauce. Garlic fried in olive oil, tomatoes, salt and pepper. Sometimes I use bacon fat or butter instead of the olive oil, and sometimes I scatter some basil into the pot at the last moment. The rest—all those green peppers and oregano and dashes of this or that, or, gasp, sugar—is all just filigree. Sometimes, filigree is exactly what's called for—but those sauces have names like puttanesca and Bolognese.

THE AUTUMN'S RICH INCREASE, the harvest, isn't exclusive to the garden patch. I recalled John Whiteside's e-mail to me about the state of the farm in autumn and how they were getting ready for winter, when they would hunt and split firewood and mend fences. Here I was, with a freezer full of beef. Here I was, ready to go out hunting again.

One of my fantasies was to make my own hot dogs. When I told my father this, he blanched.

"Hot dogs? Seriously?" He wondered why I didn't want to make something profound.

Hot dogs aren't fancy, and yet, they are difficult. David Chang, owner and chef at his Momofuku restaurants, wrote in his cookbook about trying to create food that seemed simple, because all the complicated procedures remain hidden.* (His book changed the way I cook more than any cookbook I've read since my first *Larousse Gastronomique*.) I love the idea of the outwardly simple but secretly complex, and what could be more in line with this concept than the hot dog?

We tend to scarf them down at the stadium or while

---

*This is one of the reasons I think David Chang might be *the* American chef. F. Scott Fitzgerald worked from the same premise. *Gatsby* was conceived to be so fully modern that no one would see its modernity at all.

standing on a city sidewalk without giving them much thought. Hot dogs, somehow, became a sort of weird culinary default—something you toss to the children during the cookout before the grown-ups eat an actual meal.

I suppose I have to say here that a lot of hot dogs suck. Some ridiculous percentage of the frankfurters sold in the world (85 percent, 98 percent? I don't know—most of them) are a horrendous concoction of fluffy filler and bits of animals that couldn't be sold unless they were thoroughly bleached and subsequently masked by super-powered sweeteners and artificial flavors. Real hot dogs, however, from a purely analytical standpoint, are a triumph. They are as complex as the best pâté, as subtle and rich and satisfying as food gets. They are as tricky as a good French sauce and as keen and deceptive as a fine bite of sushi. Am I pushing too hard? What, in the American pantheon of immigrant food, compares? There are other foods worthy of celebration, and I don't mean to discount them, but what else is quite as difficult to get right? If you were to have, instead of a chili cook-off, a homemade hot dog contest, how many contestants would you get?

They are an emulsified beef sausage with a complex array of aromas, and they snap when you bite into them. I wanted to make them.

In Michael Ruhlman and Brian Polcyn's *Charcuterie*, I read that "hot dogs derive their distinctive flavor primarily from garlic, paprika, beef fat and smoke."

What's interesting right away is that beef fat is usually abjured in favor of pork fat. Beef fat is . . . well, it's just weird. It doesn't always taste right; it doesn't always melt right. You know that watery, greasy smell that fills your kitchen when you brown the meat for tacos? That's beef fat. There's a reason recipes start with "brown a pound of beef and drain it." Not so with hot dogs. Hot dogs want beef fat.

The next key thing they taught me was that the "ground meat is salted for a day to develop the myosin protein that helps give the hot dog a good bind and a good bite."* They suggested short ribs to make the sausages, but I like my short ribs, and I had 160 pounds of ground beef in my freezer. I'd watched it being ground, and I'd already made some chili and from looking at the way the beef acted while browning, I could tell that it was plenty fatty enough. Twenty percent seemed right about where the meat was at.

I'd learned that the reason my breakfast sausage didn't coalesce, the reason it always seemed more like breakfast *burger* than breakfast *sausage*, was because of the way the meat had been chopped (in the food processor). If you want meat to stretch and bind to itself, you have to actu-ally grind it. This is due to the same myosin proteins that were developed by salting the meat overnight. Mixing the sausage in a stand mixer (or vigorously by hand) will do

---

*I followed this instruction without understanding it until I found an article titled "Influence of Salt and Pyrophosphate on Bovine Fast and Slow Myosin S1 Dissociation from Actin" by Qingwu W. Shen and Darl R. Swartz in which I read that "myosin is the major functional protein in muscle foods (Fukazawa, Hashimoto & Yasui, 1961a; Fukazawa, Yasui & Hashimoto, 1961b). It functions as the primary water and protein binding agent as well as fat holding protein in products (Acton, Ziegler & Burge, 1983; Asghar, Samejima & Yasui, 1985; Hamm, 1986). In meat without added salt, myosin has limited functionality because it is constrained within the thick filaments of the myofibrils. It must be released and/or re-organized within the muscle matrix for its functionality to come to the fore. The addition or injection of salt and/or pyrophosphate (PPi) into meat facilitates extraction of myosin from the thick filament of the A-band, which results in the swelling of myofibrils and increased water holding capacity of meat (Offer & Trinick, 1983; Xiong, Lou, Harmon, Wang & Moody, 2000b)." Got it?

the same. It's all about binding the proteins in the meat so that the texture becomes sausage-like.

Emulsified sausage doesn't lend itself to slapdash kitchen improvisation, so I followed the recipe religiously. I weighed the beef and added the proper measures of spices and salts. (I measured them! I used a scale! Typically, I simply pinch and sprinkle.) I chilled when they told me to and ground through frozen tools. Then, as suggested, I did what Ruhlman calls a "quenelle test." I don't think he means that you have to make a quenelle: quenelles are classically formed by moving two or three tablespoons of a paste between two dinner spoons, rolling the food over on itself until you've made a shape reminiscent of a madeleine cookie.* All Ruhlman means is that one should spoon out a bit of the food and cook it in a pan to taste if it's right before you go through the process of stuffing it into casings.

I did a quenelle test and fried it in a small skillet. It was bouncy, garlicky. It tasted like a frankfurter. I was excited. I probably smacked the table, or my forehead. Hot damn! I'd made hot dogs!

But I hadn't. I'd only made the paste that becomes a hot dog. If I wanted sausages—or in this case, hot dogs—that look and act like what everyone calls a hot dog, I'd have to stuff it in a casing and make it into links.

One of the constant challenges—much touched upon here, I realize—is ending up with not just an approximation of a cornichon, or a cheese that was like Camembert, but creating the actual thing. I want the food I make to actually *be* better than store-bought.

---

*Reminiscent of a madeleine—you didn't think we'd make it all the way through a food book without the requisite nod to Proust, did you?

I didn't think putting the meat into casings would be too difficult. I've watched people do it many times, and it seemed straightforward. I watched refresher videos about it to make sure that I grasped what was going to happen, and it looked as if nothing could be easier. The tool is certainly straightforward: my stuffer is a cast-iron curved tube with a lever that pushes meat out of an elongated stainless-steel funnel. I purchased it years ago, but it stayed in its box in the basement. Whatever enthusiasm I'd been chasing when I got it had passed. I set it up and read what there was of a manual to make sure I wasn't missing anything. I wasn't. Put the meat in the chamber and push down on the lever, making the meat slide into the casings that you've fit over the funnel. (Sliding the casings over the funnel is only the first slippery, sexy action ripe with phallic imagery in what is, really, a parade of slippery, sexy moments ripe with phallic imagery.)

The meat-paste-that-would-be-hot-dogs was thick and tacky and pink, and I globbed it into the chamber after the requisite period of chilling it down. (Everything must be cold all the time while stuffing sausages, especially emulsified sausages such as hot dogs. I chilled the pieces of the stuffer, too, just as I'd chilled the pieces of the grinder while I ground the mix together.)

Casings can be artificial (yuck), but most come from various parts of the digestive tract of animals. Hog casings are from pig intestines and make sausages the size of bratwurst or fresh Italians. Beef bungs are from the cow's cecum, a small cul-de-sac between the large and small intestines, full of digestive bacteria. Sheep casings are the smallest. I found my casings at the Thruway Sporting Goods in Walden, New York, where hunters buy grinders and seasonings for their game. The casings came in a little pouch, like chewing tobacco, and were packed in salt. They smelled bad and were stiff and crinkled. After I soaked them in a few changes of water, they became soft and flexible. I ran water through them, too, like a hose, and they didn't smell at all when it was time to use them.

I got everything set, and I pushed down on the lever. Nothing happened. I pushed again. It didn't budge. I pushed really hard, and meat started to slide up past the plunger that was supposed to be pushing it forward. Not quite undaunted, but not yet daunted, I pushed harder. Meat shot out of the back of the chamber and splattered all over the cabinet behind me. I poked and prodded in the chamber—air pocket? I pushed again, and again nothing. This went on and on—Max versus the immovable meat paste—until I had the sausage stuffer on the floor, pushing down on the lever so hard that I was grunting. At some point, I didn't even care if I got meat into the casing. I just wanted to move meat through the chamber, and I was hitting it, stepping on it, and trying to think of a way to create a kind of big lasso-like cinch knot that would squeeze the lever down. Maybe I could tie the other end of the rope to my truck. Flecks and smears of meat coagulated, crusting on the cabinets, the table, and the sink. I couldn't do it. I couldn't make it work. This was a sausage nonstuffer. By now, the meat was too warm. In a disgusted fury I packed the meat-paste-that-would-not-be-hot-dogs into a plastic bag and shoved it into the freezer, where it remains.

The next day, still seething, I tried to figure out what I had done wrong. Reading recipes for emulsified sausages, I came across one for boudin blanc, the French white sausage made with chicken and pork, seasoned with quatre épices (a French spice mix of allspice, cloves, black pepper, and cinnamon), and bound with milk and eggs. I hadn't had one in years. What's more, I had a few pheasants in the freezer. The thought of pheasant boudin blanc got me over my fury. Maybe what I needed was a different sausage.

I mixed together equal parts of pork butt and pheasant, and after I ground them finely, I put them in the food processor with eight eggs and plenty of milk, the spices, and a touch of flour. It was creamy and smooth. The quenelle test proved positive.

I used hog casings.

This time, the process worked exactly as it should. The meat went into the chilled chamber, and when I pressed the lever, it slid out of the tube and into the casing, unspooling casing as it went. I twisted the links as they filled and coiled up a pile of them on the stainless-steel table. Then I poached them.

I had some leftover mix, which I slipped into ring forms and smoked. We ate the patties over apples and onions roughly chopped and sautéed with bacon. The boudin blanc was delicate and delicious. I'd hit the mark with the seasoning; the sausage was autumnal and had that great double whammy of being light and rich at the same time, like perfect soufflé. Rachael and West enjoyed the dinner, but they couldn't have known what it meant to me. I was redeemed.

Moving forward with my harvest experiments, I chopped up two heads of cabbage from the last issue of the CSA to make them into sauerkraut. The difference between homemade sauerkraut and store-bought sauerkraut is the difference between playing that video game called *Rock Band* and being in a band. I seasoned mine with horseradish and garlic, and tossed in a couple of juniper berries. It bubbled and stank up the kitchen for a while—it goes through a phase, like a lot of fermentations, where it doesn't smell very good. This phase passes, and what you are left with is tart, acidic, and complicated. It's fulfilling in a way that vinegar-brined cabbage in plastic bags in the grocery store never could approach. In the process of tamping it down into the big glass jar that served as its fermentation crock, I solved a years-long kitchen puzzle.

I opened the drawer to look for a tool suitable for tamping, and there before my eyes was a sauerkraut tamper I hadn't known I had. It came from Rachael's grandmother. She was Polish and had lived in Hamtramck, Michigan, which was a Polish enclave in the middle of Detroit during her time. The tamper was a metal disk about a quarter of an inch thick, punched through with small holes and screwed to a metal rod with a wooden handle. Rachael's *dzidzia* (pronounced judgie—*dzidzia* is the Polish-American word for *grandpa*) had made it. He made everything. I never knew him in person, but I have grown to know him through the collection of metal files, crimps, and snips that I inherited from him, and I can only say that I wish he'd lived long enough to sit in the basement with me over cans of beer, fabricating tools. Some of what he made looked improvised. This tamper, I'd assumed, was a very poor interpretation of a potato masher. When I opened the drawer on sauerkraut day, I finally saw it for what it was.

I called Rachael at work: *Did Granny used to make her own sauerkraut?*

"All the time. Good grief, she was *Polish*."

You know that terrible potato-masher thing? That's a sauerkraut tamper.

We laughed. *Sorry, Dzidzia—I'll never underestimate you again.*

Rachael walked in the door that evening, sharp and professional in her high heels and black suit. West ran to her, and while they hugged their evening hellos, she took in a whiff of air.

To my delight, she proclaimed, "Wow, it smells like Granny's kitchen in here."

CHAPTER TWELVE

A Cow Is Not Always Black and White

I FELT IMMENSE SATISFACTION at having made it through to the other side of autumn—the freezer was packed, the jars were lined up, things were cured and ready. Even my catastrophes didn't bother me. The paste-that-would-be-hot-dogs was wadded into a corner of the freezer, but I'd tried, and I knew it tasted good. I felt like I could figure out how to get it into casings.

I'd flopped on making a bresaola, too. I had worked carefully with the four-pound eye round (a big hunk of Bubbles), and I'd followed the recipe, but I'd blown it. Halfway through hanging it, I'd taken it out and weighed it. Cured meat is ready when it has lost about 30 percent of its original water weight. It wasn't there yet, but it smelled clean, sparkly with clove and allspice, like a dark jam or a mince pie. There was a lot of pepper on the nose and a little bacon (from the pink salt). It was firm, compact, and ruby red, but it wasn't ready. When I next pulled it, it had lost 27 percent of its weight, which is close enough to done. It had some nonthreatening white and greenish mold on it, which poofed spores all over my kitchen like a stomped puffball mushroom when I unwrapped the cheesecloth. I scrubbed the mold off and rinsed the outside with a little vinegar. The meat smelled of funky socks. Not the thick, heady, stinky-cheese smell of good ham but rather the sharp, tangy, and deep smell of rot and disease. I was shaken. This was four pounds of my steer, after all. Russell and Rachael were both in the kitchen at the unveiling. At first, Rachael seemed to press herself into the corner of the room, like a schoolgirl who hadn't read the assignment hoping she could make herself invisible so she wouldn't be called on. When she realized that Russell and I both intended to *eat* it, she protested. Loudly. We were morons. She wanted nothing to do with this. She hoped our life insurance payments were up-to-date. Russell and I ate a thin slice. We nibbled for a moment, trying to decipher what was going on. It was awful, but we ate some more.

"Oh, come *on!*" cried Rachael. "This is how you two spend your time, isn't it? This is what you do while I'm at work? Jackasses."

In the name of science.

It was terrible. It was pungent, with certain spices (juniper, especially) carried aloft and heightened by the acrid, high flavor of decomposition while others seemed to have disappeared entirely. All that was left of the pepper was the harsh, white pepper heat, just a hot dusty note that poked out while something tannic and abrasive covered the palate like ground glass.

It wasn't even the first time I'd made bresaola. It was only the first time I'd tried it by the book. In the past, I'd thrown some salt on an eye of round, stuck it in the fridge, and after it was firm to the touch, I'd hung it under the eaves wrapped in cheesecloth. Sometimes I'd rub it with fennel or thyme—straightforward flavors that play well with beef. I hadn't known about the 30 percent weight-loss rule; I'd just figured that when it felt firm, it was done. My improvised cured beef had worked every time. This piece I'd made into garbage.

This bothered me, but again, I'd tried. Fail again, fail better.

The sticky problem with the ruined bresaola was that I'd slated it for Thanksgiving dinner, as part of the opening volley of charcuterie that we'd eat family style, while sipping aperitifs.

Thanksgiving had become a big deal.

That's not fair to say. It's always been a big deal around here. It's a holiday dedicated to *food*, after all. It's meant to be a *feast*. Thanksgiving is right up our street.

I'd added gravitas to the holiday by trying to set it up as a tidy closing scene for this book, for there's no real way to end a book about me in the kitchen. It's not as if I'm going to stop cooking. It wasn't as if, having eaten nothing but cats for a year (because there are too many cats), we were going to return to eating TV dinners. So I had this idea that I'd close on a big Thanksgiving table, with all my friends gathered around and a menu that really brought home all I'd learned, all I'd thought about.

We rented a lodge up the road that would easily absorb our numbers, and we spread out tasks among the attendees. Candace and Evelyn decorated. Paige brought games and activities for the kids. Russell got firewood. Sharr made dessert. Everyone brought wine. I cooked.

Cooking turned out to be a tricky proposition, considering there wasn't a kitchen at the lodge, but I solved it with steam tables and a portable burner.

The menu:

Not bresaola, but Benton's ham—no complaints there—
and home-cured duck prosciutto served family style, with
drinks.

Lobster salad with homemade mascarpone cheese
instead of mayo—Thomas Keller thought of that; it's
fantastic.

Soup of potatoes and kale (both from our garden), with
cream.

Pheasant boudin blanc made with birds I'd shot in North
Dakota, served with apples and Benton's bacon.

Braised short rib of Bubbles, with homemade onion
marmalade and good Neal's Yard Stilton, on homemade
sourdough.

Finally, smoked ballotine of turkey garnished with
home-pickled cranberries and home-pickled mustard seeds
and served next to roasted brussels sprouts from the last
CSA issue.

For dessert, Sharr made mountains of donuts. Far too
many donuts. You shouldn't put that many donuts near
people, especially children. They were delectable: some
were topped with bacon crumbles and bourbon glaze;
some were glazed with caramel and sprinkled with big
flakes of Maldon salt; some were made with pumpkin and
pie spices.

Russell built a handsome fire. The table was covered
with burlap and decorated with pomegranates, gourds,
hurricane lamps, twigs, and the long, wispy tail feathers of
rooster pheasants. The kids ran and tackled one another
and wore feather headdresses and formed, at some point,
a society sworn to loyalty and secrecy, inscribing their
names on a plank.

We had a lot of fun, and I count it as a success, though
perhaps I worked a little too hard. Neither was the timing

perfect: it's difficult to pace a dinner service for twenty-odd people when I also wanted to sit down with them to eat, laugh, and watch the firelight sparkle in my friends' eyes. We all cleaned together, sweeping up and stacking the chairs. I passed around a bottle of excellent peach eau-de-vie from Rory's distillery in Colorado.

Eau-de-vie straight from the bottle, clear and hot and robust while still tasting of the soft, squishy fruit that made it, was a great way to end the meal, but I realized soon enough that I hadn't found an ending to this book. Because everything I wanted to do, everything I'd learned and changed, I would keep on doing. To draw the curtain and say that it ended at a dinner party is arbitrary.

A few weeks later, I was up early, pulling on my hunting boots and grabbing my gear. I drove an hour and a half to the north, to a big stretch of land owned by a friend. Above his farmhouse is a field, which used to be in alfalfa. They hadn't leased it that year, and the meadow was wild and tangly. I'd walked it earlier in the fall, and I'd seen the deer paths and the beds where the whitetails spent the night. There was scat everywhere. I tucked myself into the edge of the woods, near a crumbling round bale of alfalfa that had been left behind two years ago. I waited and I watched until I was chilled to the bone and hungry enough to be fantasizing not about food in general but about specific dishes. I dreamed of a bowl of ramen and every ingredient I'd want in the bowl. There is where I'd tuck the square of nori, the slice of pork belly, the egg.

I didn't see any deer.

Soon, the ramen bowl in my imagination was running parallel with a simple dream of sitting in my truck with the heat blasting, holding my hands over the heater vents. I stayed still and I waited and I watched. I remembered that I had a novel—*The Master and Margarita*, by Mikhail Bulgakov—on my phone. I slipped it out of my pocket and waited some more, reading and wondering who read while waiting for deer. I bet it's more common than one would think. My gun stayed in my lap all day. I didn't get a deer, but I was happy.

Happy because I was trying, attempting things because they are worth trying. I'd broken down the impulse to hesitate, to accept the status quo. I wasn't just attempting things I knew I was good at, or things for which I was prepared.

I hadn't fried pig ears, for example, but I wanted to eat some. My market was all out of ears. The butcher chuckled and said, "Actually, I have some, but they're still attached."

I'll take the head.

"I can cut them off if you'd like me to; it's no big deal."

No, really. I'll take it.

Walking through a grocery store with a pig's head in your cart makes you an instant celebrity, but not exactly in a nice way. People stop and look, brimming with a cocktail of curiosity and repulsion. They want to ask, but they are nervous. With a pig's head in my cart, I got a glimpse of what it must feel like to be Larry Flynt, the golden wheelchair-driving publisher of *Hustler*. A woman by the green peppers couldn't restrain herself.

"Is that a pig's head?"

It is.

"What are you going to do with that?" At once she began retreating. She wanted to know, but she did not want to talk to the bearded man with a head in his shopping cart. I answered as she stepped away, walking slowly backward and holding a bell pepper between us like a cross to ward off vampires.

I'm going to make headcheese.

Of course I can make headcheese. Why wouldn't I? I did, and it was delightful: porky and rich, suspended in chilled broth from the slow boil with bay leaves and chile flakes, dashed with apple cider vinegar. We ate it for lunch with grainy mustard and crusty bread.

One afternoon, Russell texted me: "If I shot a squirrel, would you cook it?"

No sooner had I shot off a reply in the affirmative than Russell was walking into the yard.

That was fast; I thought we were speaking hypothetically.

"I'd already shot him. The squirrel was on the ground when I texted you."

We cleaned him—again I made Russell do most of the dirty work, pulling the skin off and gutting. I just neatened the animal up and got him ready for the pot. I browned the squirrel in bacon fat and braised it in red wine. Squirrel is delicious—similar to rabbit, but better and more flavorful. I can't wait until we have a few and can make shredded squirrel over pappardelle.

The squirrel was a spontaneous bit of fun. Some adventures are more calculated. When a friend of mine named Bekah Tighe and I took over a local bar—a great bar, the local dive, with a lingering reputation for sketchiness it no longer deserves—it was for a lark. We made a pop-up restaurant called 5&10—every drink was five bucks, and every plate ten. We designed the menu together, and while she led the kitchen, Rachael and I tended bar. We served fried tripe, chilled octopus dressed with olives, and a hanger steak with a Vidalia onion and mint chimichurri. We slung classic cocktails, like the Aviation, and inventions of my own, like the Cin and Smoke—mezcal with chipotle cinnamon bitters that I'd made, agave syrup, and lime.

We were over fire-code capacity in no time, and we stayed that way until we ran out of everything. Those weeds were deep. If you haven't worked in a restaurant— or I suppose lived with someone who does—you don't know what it means to be "in the weeds." If you look it up, you'll get a vanilla definition about a restaurant worker struggling because the business has surpassed his capacity. That is technically accurate but evokes a level of stress akin to a perilous moment in traffic during the evening commute. The weeds are more like three and a half hours on one hundred–degree pavement in the Indianapolis 500. Toby Cecchini wrote in his book *Cosmopolitan*, "There is something morbidly fascinating about hitting that tipping point and seeing what happens to everyone in the place. This is, perhaps not surprisingly, when we work best, with all cylinders clicking."

5&10 was a very individual sort of deep fun. Working that hard next to Rachael, cracking each other up and pausing for shots of whiskey, is one of my favorite things to do. I love it when we're in over our head, using everything we've got.

This fun, this high, is connected to the root motivation behind why I always say yes, why I always think I can do it myself. Can I make Camembert? Raise a steer? Put up enough tomatoes to see us through until the next harvest? The answer is always yes. Of course I can.

These are grand gestures, I realize: feasts, headcheese, squirrel. I find great pleasure outside of extravagance as well, and there were simpler expressions of my newfound confidence. Working on a menu for a dinner, for instance, I led myself to a dish of my own sour bread, pan toasted in olive oil, topped with shiitakes and fromage blanc. Fromage blanc is a farmer's cheese, spreadable and slightly crumbly, very fresh. I didn't have any, and I didn't want to drive the half hour to the closest place I could think of that might have some. So I moved on, momentarily thinking I'd cook something else, before I caught myself. I was almost sure I knew how to make fromage blanc. I scanned some books to be sure, and then I did it.

I picked this instinct up from my folks. Years ago, an old girlfriend of my parents told me that my mom's first instinct has always been to make things herself. I can see my mom and her friend, from all the slivers of stories I've heard. They are young women, eating whole-wheat raisin bread with walnuts and Neufchâtel cheese at Chock Full o'Nuts in midtown Manhattan. They'd window-shop or walk through Macy's to the food store in the basement, and when they saw something they liked, my mom's friend would want to buy it. My mom would look at it, think about it for a second, and announce that she could make it. She did it just the other day, in fact, when I showed her my new butter keeper—a cup that slides upside down into a little crock with some water in it and keeps the butter cool and fresh. She looked at it, held it in her hands, and said she'd make herself one. (She's an accomplished potter, so this isn't a stretch for her, but I think she'd have said that no matter what.)

Within this impulse to try is the classic inclination of the amateur. What Sandor Ellix Katz smartly calls the "disempowering cult of specialization" has done what it can to stifle the will to try things, to try for the pleasure of doing. It's a shame, because that's where the fun is. Surely specialization and expertise are satisfying—it's good to know that only you have the key to your silo—but it is equally, differently satisfying to try things out, to paint on Sundays because you like to think about light, or to take over a bar because you like mixing drinks and you think you might be fast enough to do it. Sometimes you'll fail, but so what? That's the great gift of being an amateur, after all.

Grantland Rice's poem "Alumnus Football" is familiar to almost everyone who speaks English because of the closing couplet, which is often misquoted. He wrote of the Great Scorer, who would ultimately judge us, and that "he writes—not that you won or lost—but HOW you played the Game." I would take it a step further and say that the first real mark would judge whether or not you stepped onto the field at all. *That's* the most important part—just being game.

I started my series of experiments, refining and fostering my DIY impulses and moving the way my family gets our food up the supply chain, closer to the source, because I'd been thinking about the new American kashrut, the new system of rules about what to eat, what's "kosher." Also, there was a cheeseburger.

One bright day in late summer, Rachael and I took West shopping for school clothes. We couldn't find anything exciting to eat for lunch, and we settled into one of the ubiquitous sit-down franchises that dot American highways, all fake antiques and nachos, the wretched final manifestation of the fern bar.

I got a burger. I don't mean to be coy or to overplay my own naiveté, but I certainly felt right then that being hungry and sitting down in a restaurant that sells a lot of burgers might be an uneventful experience. What came out of the kitchen caught me off guard. What *was* it, exactly? How could ground beef be so spongy? What part of a cow is frothy and light pink? No part I wanted to eat. With every bite, I fell deeper into the nightmarish whirlpool of my own imagination. I thought of all the things that happen far away from the plate, all the processes that are disguised and forgotten. The pink-slime headlines were still a couple of years in our future, so I don't know what spawned my visions of a meat-flecked skeleton being hosed with some sort of high-pressure device, like the one I use to clean the boards of my deck, and a trough catching a slurry of connective tissue, ligaments, nerves, and blood vessels. That slurry would be whipped into an emulsion and squished into patties, sprayed with artificial grill flavor, heated and plated and put in front of me as if it were food. I can't eat that. I sure as hell don't want my family eating it.

It was revolting. I rejected it.

Jim Harrison wrote in his book *The Raw and the Cooked,* "It is no fun to butcher your own geese, but the supermarket birds are far too lean, and then neither is it any fun to live a life where all the dirty work, the realities, are left to someone else because of our purchasing power." I know what he means when he says it's no fun. Ultimately, it's just another chore. But when I look back upon time spent plucking birds (or canning tomatoes, or digging out weeds), it feels fun. I don't remember the tedium of plucking out stubborn feathers any more than the prick of a thistle is the salient memory of clearing a garden patch. What I take away is a feeling of accomplishment and of having done something.

Throughout my attempts at deep foodie DIY production, I have at times overdone it, gone too far, and ended up in the wilds or the weeds and slightly lost or overcome. I've had, also, some real successes. By essaying more than I could comfortably achieve, I've found myself clicking on all cylinders, working to the best of my capabilities. I will remain very proud of my seawater risotto, for instance, and my first pheasant.

To reach always for such moments, however, would be like pining for Icarus's wax wings as if I'd never seen Brueghel's painting of how that's going to end (or read Auden's poem about it). In the Dutch master's painting, we see of our subject only two flailing legs; the rest of him has already drowned. There's a ploughman at work in the foreground, and a shepherd in the middle, and an angler with a good view of the splash. None of them seem to care. In Ovid's account, they stand in awe, as if the gods were approaching, but in the painting, they are aloof. They've got things to do. The ship, sailing right by the boy who fell into the sea, couldn't have missed the sight, but the ship had somewhere to go, and on it went. Most of the time, we aren't in the weeds or at the top of our game. We might be stretched out, but we aren't redlining. Most of the time, we are simply cooking dinner. The truth is, I am—we are—more like the ship sailing by Icarus as he slips into the ocean than we are like the overachieving winged boy plummeting on account of his pride.

What to make of that? I wondered. To strive and to know that I'll fail. To hit hard, knowing that I can't knock anything out. Is it all just a story about a cock and a bull?

Last week, I stood at my stove while West did his homework. He had to choose five words from a set and use them in a sentence (the sentences had to be at least seven words long, so there was a lot of counting on fingers as he worked out his ideas). This is a ritual moment, exactly where you will find us most days of the week—West at the kitchen table with a pencil and a notebook,

me at the stove with a wooden spoon, and Rachael riding
the train home from work. If all goes right—I'd say we bat
about .550—she walks in the door just as we're finishing
homework and dinner.

I was making a simple gumbo into which I was going
to shred duck from a confit I'd made. I was browning
roux and sweating the Cajun trinity of bell pepper, onion,
and celery. I had a broth bubbling on the back burner. I
chopped some garlic and told West that he could not say
that something was "very, very, very blue" to achieve
his word count. He laughed. He knew that. He was just
kidding.

His word was *always*.

"I've got it," he announced.

Hit me, I said, turning to face him.

"A cow is not always black and white."